Once Upon A Farm

Through The Eyes Of A Wife

Written by **Lois Stark**

Illustrated by **Paula Wouts-Hanson**

Down-To-Earth Publishing

First Edition

Library of Congress Catalog Number: 92-72893

ISBN: 0-9633478-3-7

For additional copies of this book, contact:

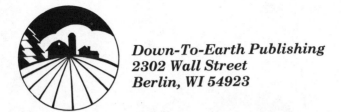

Down-To-Earth Publishing
2302 Wall Street
Berlin, WI 54923

Printed in the United States of America by Palmer Publications, Inc.
Amherst, WI 54406

Dedication

To those who believe in farming as a way of making a living as well as a way of life—those American farmers are the richest resource this country has—now being mined to extinction.

And to the dignity of those farmers—born of honesty, self-respect, determination, and hard work. The dignity that is generations of farm families caring for the land, the crops, the animals, and each other. The dignity that founded a nation, guided its growth, and will—or the absence of it will—determine its future.

Contents

Acknowledgements

I am grateful to the farm and the land, and all the good people living thereon, who in sharing with me this way of life inspired many of these pages.

Especially my husband, Henry, who edited each essay for content, and tolerated the dining table more often piled with books and papers than with food. He also introduced, encouraged, and then maintained my relationship with the computer.

Many thanks to Sue Bartlett for her kind encouragement and skillful copy editing.

Deep appreciation to Paula Wouts-Hanson, a former farm girl, who expresses it all so well in her sketches.

Henry and Lois.

Introduction

The cow had died of milk fever. My husband was depressed. Later that day, in the spring of 1987, he talked with a neighbor who was also feeling helpless after not being able to save his top cow from the same misfortune.

My husband instantly felt better, not because the neighbor's cow died, but because he realized he was not in this alone. This led me to question how many other farmers needed to share. It prompted the start of my column, "The Farmer's Wife," which has appeared ever since in the *Berlin Journal Newspapers*.

This book contains some of my efforts during this period. Farmers and their families are torn between technology and tradition, having a way of life and making a living, keeping their sons on the farm and giving them an "easier" way. The essays share the sorrows, fears, and frustrations, as well as the joys, satisfaction, and pride of our farm life.

I seek to inform farm and urban folk, since many urban folk don't realize how bad it is on the farm, and many farm folk don't appreciate how good it is.

Those who grew up on a farm and left, may be reminded what it is like to press your face to the velvet cheek of a newborn calf, to work up a sweat in the hay mow, and to be in touch with God once again.

These pages record and reflect on an era that is being destroyed by uncertainties and regulations, and by the ill-fated trend to expansion in pursuit of better returns.

P. WOUTS-HANSON

Sunup To Sundown

Making Hay

The sweetest smell on earth to a dairyman is of fresh cut hay. If sunshine had a smell, I think it would be like that of drying alfalfa. The stems send forth a delicate sweet herb-like essence. I wonder if it gives the cows the same high it does me. When passing a field, I savor the aroma, inhaling long and deep.

Whereas one of the worst smells is that of rotting foliage, especially hay. When rain soaks drying hay, the most-perfect food for a ruminant animal is quickly reduced to a soggy, rope-like mass with considerably fewer nutrients. The rank stench can make a man lose his appetite, not only because of the smell, but because of the loss it represents to him. We've had some of both smells this year.

"Should I cut?" my husband asks. "They say there is a 30 percent chance of showers tomorrow night. I hate to take a chance, but the hay needs to be cut. It's getting stemmy."

"Cut some, but not a lot," I reply, hopefully not commit-ting myself too much.

Henry always asks my advice, but I don't think he values my opinion that much. He just doesn't want to carry the load alone, when unexpected clouds come up like gang-busters and soak eight acres of windrowed bounty.

The weatherman on TV casually smiles and jests, "That front moved through a little faster than we expected, but we were only 24 hours off."

Twenty-four hours can mean a lot of money during haying season.

"I should have cut more," Henry admonishes himself, if we are fortunate enough to get in all that was cut without getting rain on it.

"I shouldn't have cut so much," he says if some gets rained on. Then he rationalizes and comforts his nerves,

1

Once Upon A Farm

"Well, we needed the rain, and the second crop will get a chance to grow now."

I'm thankful that after many years of playing this game with the weatherman, he has learned to find pluses among the minuses.

There are years of memories of racing with thunderheads. When I was a girl it was "pulling rope." My job was to pull the rope back each time after the men set the huge fork in the loose load and then urged the horses to pull it up to the mow. We really moved when the skies darkened.

Methods changed and by the time I was married I became a "baler." When I had to wait for an empty wagon I lay on my back in the shade of the full load, and watched the freedom of the clouds above, or observed the diligence of a beetle weaving its way through the stubble. Always, my eye scanned the horizon as I guided my machines up and down the neat rows. Sometimes a strong wind would precede the rain, and I'd do some real maneuvering to catch the wind-rows while the wind twisted them as a snake. I pushed the gas lever all the way up and flipped the tractor in the highest gear that could take it; praying that the knotter on the baler wouldn't rebel against working with such haste—and yes, that I wouldn't run out of twine—not now.

Today, even as the rain came down, I kept going as long as the baler would take the damp stuff. Henry or one of the "helping hands" raced out to the field to get the load in the shed quickly. I followed with the baler and joined them in the shed. We stood there; our wet clothes plastered to our bodies with a mixture of greenish chaff, rain and sweat. We watched the torrents come down, feeling limp and helpless.

This year we've also had to race with the weevil. It's the first time we have seen the ugly green worm in our fields.

"Something's eating our hay," Henry exclaims one day in disbelief. He promptly phones an agronomist to see if his suspicions are correct.

"Cut it as soon as you can. The sooner you cut, the more of it you will get before the weevils do," was the advice. "If it doesn't 'green up' after you cut, they are still at work and you will have to spray."

We did notice that a 10 acre field, lying right next to other

infected fields, had no weevil at all. Why? Henry recalled
burning this field in early April because of all the debris
from the lodged oats crop from last year.

Did the burning kill all the eggs and larvae?

Perhaps we can get a $20,000 grant from the government
to study the situation.

June, 1987

*Henry unloads hay bales into the elevator which carries
them into the mow.*

A Rainy Day And Nothing To Do?

It was raining hard as I went to the milkhouse. Mixing
the milk at the sink for the calves' morning feeding, I
noticed someone had splattered the wall with muddy
streaks. The milkhouse door was marked with dirty hand
smudges. The waste basket overflowed, and my boot slid on
the accumulation of lime and milkfat on the floor. Grey
scum edged the sink. The gloom of the day made all appear

even more messy and dismal. I couldn't work outside, so I
set to work sudsing and scraping and spraying.

An hour later I trudged back to the house. As I changed
clothes in the back entry, I was irritated by the winter boots,
vests, and caps still lining the walls. "No work outside
today," they seemed to be chanting at me, "time to clean us
and put us away."

"Not today, not today," I chanted back. Today was the
day to write out bills. Besides there were plenty of other jobs
on my list waiting for a rainy day.

Walking through the kitchen I noticed my favorite violet
leaning cock-eyed over the edge of its pot, and made a men-
tal note to re-pot plants later in the day.

And then there was that basket of "touch up" ironing and
pile of knee-less jeans at the end of the sewing machine
table. However, the ironing board had purebred applications
stacked on it, put there so I wouldn't forget to send them in
on time. Better do that today, since it's raining. How I hated
all these "odds and ends" jobs.

Henry came in for breakfast. It was still raining. There
would be no baling hay today. Aha, I thought, this is a good
time to put in my order for fixing the bird feeder and getting
those calves dehorned and vaccinated.

"Are you kidding?" His question was my answer. "We
have to work on that inoculant applicator today. Couldn't
get it to work. Need to have it ready for the hay as soon as
the weather clears."

"How long will it take?" I meekly asked, still hoping.

"Could be an hour, could be all day. Then I need to get
some parts for the sprayer. Have an appointment with the
accountant at ten-thirty, and I'm behind in my book work. If
I don't get that workshop cleaned up pretty soon we're not
going to be able to find anything. I've been putting it off for
a rainy day—guess because it's a job I don't like."

The phone rang. "Caught you in the house today," the
salesman's voice blatted. "Raining, and nothing to do,
right?"

"Wrong," Henry answered, rolling his eyes.

After breakfast I went back to the barn for some breeding
dates I needed for the purebred applications. Dennis, the

herdsman hailed me. "Can you help me bring some heifers in?"

He had decided it was a good day to move cows around and bring in the springing heifers, so when he got busy haying they would know their stanchions. We spent a good half hour with the cantankerous beasts. Their bellies being full of green marsh grass, they saw no reason why they should come into a strange, closed-in place.

Dennis wipes cleansing teat dip from the cow's udder in preparation for milking. Cows have to be milked every day, even on rainy days!

Thinking that maybe Dennis would have time to pound a nail in the bird feeder, I placed my order again.

"Well maybe later," he answered. "But first I have to fix that barn door before the painters come, and the free stalls need cleaning. The corn planter has to be pressure washed and put away, and the truck has a flat tire and . . . "

"Never mind. It can wait," I cut in, retreating to the house before he had a chance to tell me about the silo unloader that broke down. It was obvious the old platform bird feeder, with its supporting feet rotting away, would have to fall flat in the path of the lawn mower before it was going to get any attention—on some rainy day.

It could rain for a month and we wouldn't get caught up, but already I was anxious for the sun to re-appear so we could do some REAL work like cultivating corn and making hay.

It wasn't raining too hard right now, and the ground was wet enough so those weeds in the asparagus bed would come out real easy.

My feet turned to the garden, escaping the ironing board—until the next rainy day!

June, 1989

Talking The Language

What's the difference between a cow and a heifer, a steer and a bull?

Because of low milk prices, dairy farmers are getting a little more press lately. I often see animals, machines, and farm procedures mis-labeled, so I thought I'd offer a condensed lesson in "farm lingo."

Let's start with the animals. A baby member of the cattle family is a **calf**. If it's a boy it's a **bull**, unless he gets castrated—then he's a **steer**. A baby girl is a **heifer**, until she has her first baby, when she becomes a cow. Even so, many dairymen will still refer to her as a heifer for most of her first lactation. I guess she has to prove herself.

Which brings us to the word, **lactation**, which is the length of time a cow produces milk after calving. Hopefully it will be 305 days, although many go 365 days or more, especially if they have not been "bred back" on time. There is some debate presently if there is more money in leaving cows "open" (unbred) for a longer time and thus getting extra milk without the expense and stress of calving; or using hormones, heat detectors, and other artificial means to try to get them bred by the usual 60 days after calving. (And some think all we have to do is milk them.)

The father is referred to as a **sire**. The mother is the **dam**. Sometimes this word is also used to describe the whole barnyard of animals.

A **cull cow** is one that is no longer paying for her room and board, so she is sent to market—quickly if you need room. She gets a reprieve if milk prices are up, feed is cheap, and you have no one to fill her spot; or if she is the wife's pet.

Now when Bessie doesn't eat, she is **off feed**. If she can't get up she is a **downer**. If she has **milk fever** it means she is not hot, but cold, with below normal body temperature. She needs calcium intravenously—fast—to get her body back in balance.

A **D.A.** is not a doctor of animals. It stands for displaced abomasum; in the farmer's own language, "twisted gut." Her stomach, in trying to re-position after calving has twisted an intestine. Surgery is necessary, the sooner the better.

Hard milk does not mean cottage cheese, although sometimes it may look like that. It is another word for **mastitis**, the dairyman's constant thorn of a problem. It's an infection of the udder caused by the introduction of bacteria, dirt, injury, or any kind of stress to the udder. Costing thousands of dollars in lost milk, treatment, and time, it's a real headache.

To **scour** does not mean to polish the milk utensils. It means the calf has diarrhea, usually yellowish and putrid smelling. With death a threatening possibility, it's another common, costly, hard-to-solve problem.

It may help you to know your "ups" and "downs" when talking to farmers: To **put hay down** is to throw it out of the mow to feed the animals. To **put hay up** is to cut, dry, and store it in the barn or silo during the summer. The **corn went down** means that wind combined with wet weather and poor root structure caused the stalks to topple—not a happy situation. The **corn is up** may mean two things: the market price is up; or the seed's new yellow-green sprout of life has pierced the earth. Either will bring smiles of elation to the corn grower.

As to equipment, a **free stall** is not something for

nothing. It's an open-ended stall for a cow to go in and out of as she pleases for "resting time." A **tie stall** is a large, comfortable, barn stall in which she is "tied" by a chain snapped onto a neck collar. The **stanchion** is a neck enclosure which allows her to get up and lie down, eat and drink, but not much more than that.

Bunk silos are not piled on top of each other, but are horizontal instead of upright, usually made with concrete walls. A **bunk feeder** is a trough, wagon, or conveyor that brings the feed to the cows. Most cows "have it made" these days.

A **honey wagon** is the term sometimes used for the long, sided wagon equipped with a moving bed to carry and spread cow manure. If the novice hired hand spreads it with the wind behind him, he soon learns how much like honey it is. Sometimes this machine is referred to as the "republican platform" (especially lately). It's also the one machine a salesman will not stand behind.

Any questions? Ask your local farm neighbor. He's always ready to talk "his language."

April, 1991

Dinner Is When?

I turned the oven off. If I kept it on much longer the baked pork chops would be hydrated bread crumbs. The potatoes had simmered as long as they could if they weren't going to end up as wallpaper paste, instead of fluffy mounds. I've learned I can keep them eatable a little longer on low heat *after* they are mashed. Many other little tricks are learned from necessity in this position of cooking for farm men.

Every prospective farm bride should take a course in "How to Keep a Meal Warm and Eatable for Two Hours." Sometimes I can understand. Having been out there myself, I know what it's like to want to finish that field or get that last bolt in place. But sometimes the delay could be avoided with a little effort or forethought. There are days I feel taken advantage of.

For the tenth time I go to the window. The custom

combine is crawling over the not-so-golden waves of grain. It seems everyone has the same problem this year. Ample early rains made the straw grow fast, but spindly. When the winds came, the grain went down and the weeds came through. Henry doesn't like to spray herbicide on oats for fear of damaging the alfalfa seedlings underneath. The hired man appears at the back door.

"Henry says I'm supposed to eat. When I'm done, he'll come in."

"Okay, come on in." I knew they wanted to keep the combine moving. The driver had his lunch in the cab with him and wouldn't be stopping.

So I put everything on the table and decide to microwave it later for Henry, wondering to myself how I ever managed before the invention of those miraculous waves.

Even at that, this is better than years earlier when I sometimes came up from the fields at the same time with the men and put out cold sandwiches or quick-fried hamburger.

Before that I often got meals balancing a whiny baby on one hip, cooking with one hand. Baby's precious hours of nap-time were used to do important work outside in the garden, cutting lawn, or washing milkers.

While waiting for Henry I do some laundry and clean a cupboard. You learn to juggle your work: little jobs around mealtimes; big jobs when you *think* you might have a few undisturbed hours.

At two o'clock I hear Henry washing in the back hall.

"Had a flat tire on the gravity box. Can I eat right away? The hay is drying fast. I'll have to bale. Dennis will have to unload the grain. Looks like rain." His sentences pile on top of each other as he drops his dirty body to a chair.

This was one of those days when eating a meal was just a nuisance no one had time for.

He's half way through a pork chop when I see black and white bodies flashing past the kitchen window. "The heifers are out!" Someone apparently didn't hook the temporary wire across the lane, or else their "sixth sense" told the young cattle the "juice" was off. They are thoroughly enjoying their excursion into forbidden areas of the yard. Like teenagers on a fling, they are kicking their heels out behind them and throwing their heads wildly.

That ends Henry's dinner. We tear out of the house. It takes us twenty minutes to get the cattle rounded up. By that time he has to go bale. I can see chores will be late tonight—and so will supper.

Dairy farmers have a choice: supper followed by milking; or milking followed by supper. Neither is ideal. Not liking to work on a full stomach, Henry has chosen the latter. It would be after eight o'clock tonight, if we were even that lucky.

Clearing the table, I put scraps in the dog bucket. A few hours later on my way to the barn, I take it out to our black lab, Snoopy, who is dancing circles around me, drooling in anticipation.

"At least I only have to feed you once a day, Snoopy, when *I* decide to."

August, 1987

Farm Wardrobe

He wore loose coveralls of white plastic that came down over yellow plastic boots and hooded his head. Green goggles covered his eyes. Was it the abominable snowman? No, just Henry getting ready to spray chemicals earlier this summer.

I don't look much better when I spray the apple trees. Picture large rubber boots over jeans and a windbreaker jacket zipped up to the neck (even when it's 90 degrees). Yellow latex covers the hands. I borrow the green goggles which sit on a paint mask over my nose. It's all topped off with a bandanna over my hair, capped by a Pioneer green visor to shield from falling spray.

Farm wardrobes are varied and interesting, designed for practicality—not looks.

The costume for unloading hay must include leg, arm, and hand protection from needle-like hay stems that can pierce the skin. You're going to sweat either way, and the salt in fresh hay cuts only makes it worse.

Apparel for milking cows needs to be loose enough to allow for a lot of bending, squatting and lifting; and should cover the shoulders if you don't like wearing cow hair. Shoes should be firm enough to protect toes that get stomped on.

I guess I wouldn't make the "best dressed list" when I feed calves. Baggy, faded jeans are tucked into Tingly boots. My dad's old blue chambray shirts are my favorite tops, covered with a sweatshirt when necessary. A bandanna worn like a skull cap secures my hair. Soon a smear of saliva appears where Dolly sucked on my arm; a brown stain stands out on my jeans where I dripped the iodine while treating a naval. Sparkle, my favorite calf, pushes me with her head and leaves the oatmeal-like slobber from her mouth across my front. I back into a fresh spot inside the pen while shaking bedding, resulting in a manure trademark on my back pocket. In spite of it all, for me, nothing brings more comfort to body or mind than this work "uniform."

Jeans are universal for men, women, and children. When my dad wore them with the bib in front and straps crossed in the back, they were called "overalls." The term is fitting, since in winter they went "over all" including long underwear and denim under-slacks.

Mom was lucky to get them into the wash once a week. "You'll wear 'em out washin' 'em," he protested. But when it was time to shock oats, then prickers found their way through the weave and he changed twice a day.

Many farmers now wear coveralls when they are sliding under machinery for repairs, working in the manure, or doing cold weather field work. It saves a little on the jean washing. Even so, I've been known to pre-wash outer garments in the milk house sink by hand, before punishing my washing machine with their grit, grease, and grime.

"Change your clothes," The farm mom hollers as soon as the kids come home from school. "Change your clothes," she admonishes her husband before he goes to town or enters "her" living room. I doubt if anyone changes clothes more often than a farmer. Since the barn smell is more penetrable than Glade and sticks better than Chanel No. 5, these clothes need to be kept for that purpose only.

The wardrobe does not have to be expensive—at least not for farm women. They often wear what their husbands no longer can or will; such as flannel shirts with the elbows out (she patches or cuts the sleeves off), saggy or holey sweatshirts, and patched jeans. The cows don't care. They'll take your attention whether you're in style or not.

"Yes, Mom," my grown daughter recently confided, "we never wanted *anyone* to see us in our barn clothes."

If clothes make the man—or woman—I'm afraid I'm never going to be a woman.

No amount of silk and sequins or fine tweeds can cover the conscience of a job poorly performed, or a dishonest business.

It's not in every wardrobe, but there is something glorious in being covered with the dirt and exhaustion of honest work—well done.

October, 1990

Picture Perfect

"Put some more Orvus soap on that brown spot on her hock," Henry commanded.

I was busy scouring Chantilly's rough hooves with a wire brush, trying to remove caked-on manure. "It won't do any good," I said. "She's got the hair rubbed off. It's like a callous."

We had the huge cow tied outside the milk house so we could reach her with a warm water hose. Henry turned it on and I stood back to survey our progress. Chantilly was a beauty, big and deep, showing dairyness, along with a perfect udder and disposition. Whenever you milked her she would swing her head back in the tie stall and lick whatever part of you she could reach.

The stud service wanted to use her picture in promoting her sire. "If you can have her clean and clipped," they said, "we'll be there at 8:30 Friday morning."

We lathered and brushed and sprayed. Before long she looked as if she had on a new dress.

"We'll put her in the pen with lots of clean straw so she doesn't get dirty again," Henry said.

That afternoon Rick Trampf, a neighbor who often shows cattle, came to clip her. "I can tell she's a good cow because her hair is fine and silky," he said.

With her whole head clipped she looked like a prima donna. Then he spent another half hour shaping her body with his clippers, leaving hair where he wanted more fullness and shaving it off where he wanted to decrease size. I didn't know there was so much art to clipping a cow!

The stud service arrived on time the next morning with a crew of five and a van full of supplies.

Their first job was to select a studio. It had to look natural and compliment the cow, yet not be so interesting as to detract from her. After considering the dried stubble on the hillside for ten minutes, they changed their mind and selected a huge lilac bush as a backdrop.

Next item: prepare the site. Henry got out the riding mower and clipped the dry grass short. This was raked into a pile to cover the wooden block that went under her front feet. Elevating the front part of her body would give her a majestic look. The camera was perched on a tripod, all focused in, ready to go.

Enter subject. Prepare for final grooming. The hair along Chantilly's backbone was sprayed with mousse, back-combed, clipped evenly with a barber's scissors, and then doused with baby powder. This made the little jag in her back-line appear perfectly straight. WHOOPS! Time for the bucket! Don't want any green manure stains down her legs. A wipe job followed. "That's why that gal had those paper towels tucked in her belt," said Henry. "She knew the time would come."

Now for the pose. "Okay, get her rump over a little closer to the camera," said the photographer, an attractive young woman in Levis. She not only commanded a good knowledge of cameras, but also of cows. She picked up Chantilly's hind leg and put it a step ahead of the other one. Back at the camera she directed, "Turn her front leg around a little. She has it toed in."

I was amazed that Chantilly left her legs where they put them. Of course Gib, the man at the halter, held a very snug grip.

"Touch her back down in front of the hip bones." Fingernails poked along her backbone caused her to lower it, just as when someone jabs a pencil in your back.

"Bert, let her see the calf." All this time the fifth helper was hiding behind the van with one of our young calves. He led it out slowly, the purpose being that Chantilly's maternal interest would perk up her ears and give a bright alert look. It did that all right. The calf leaped and bawled with joy. Chantilly lunged forward. My heart sank.

"So, she likes the calf," the photographer stated calmly, grabbing a leg again. It was back to base one.

Finally all was set again. "Stand back—let me have her. Okay, Bert, a little slower this time."

The calf peeked out. The ears went up. The shutter clicked.

"Get her head higher, Gib. Stretch her out."

Click.

"Got her."

I released the breath I was holding.

When the perfect picture came in the mail a week later, I thought about the day again. Maybe with five attendants, a little spray paint, mousse, and a few props—even I could look good in a picture!

August, 1988

This photo is the result of Chantilly's session with the photographer.

Planning A Day Off

For once no cow turned up sick or decided to calve just when we wanted to go away. I finished feeding the calves early with no problems.

It looked like we would get an early start on our day off in the middle of the week. That can happen once in a while on the farm this time of year—a breather after getting the grain in, and before starting third crop hay and corn harvest. After a big push is over, you reward yourself with a day off.

Dennis, our herdsman, had scheduled a "shopping for school" trip with his young children, and we had a date with friends on the waters of Green Lake.

Heading to the house I saw the green chopper parked in front of the work shop. Oh, no! Anything parked there meant it had trouble. The resounding bang and clang of metal upon metal affirmed my fears. Something broke.

I have learned that under such circumstances it is not wise to march up to the men and demand, "What did you do now?" No, you walk gingerly behind them, hoping that during a break in the banging an explanation will escape from their clenched teeth.

Henry was trying to release a crippled piece of metal that once was a paddle. I decided something had gone through the blower. In the dust underneath the machine lay a ½ by 6 inch wagon pin. "That's what did it," Henry said bitterly. "Someone lost it in the field during first crop and I found it."

The chopping machine had picked up the pin. The auger took it into the blower where it badly nicked a chopping knife, and then got caught between a paddle and the housing, putting ugly gouges in both.

Do things ever go as planned?

Henry jumped into the pickup and sped off to town to get a new paddle, while Dennis kept banging away. We needed this machine to chop the green alfalfa for the cow's feed today. They were already lining up at the barnyard fence, bellering complaints about the delay in their breakfast. We could throw them some dried hay, but the alfalfa needed

15

cutting and we didn't really care to upset their diet or production just before D.H.I.A. production test day.

What could I do to help? Not much—except stay out of the way and not ask any dumb questions.

I phoned our friends to tell them we would be a little late—again. Henry's breakfast would be skipped, so I made up an egg sandwich he could eat on the way.

The pickup returned. I quickly went to the window. Good, he had the part. In the bathroom I laid out his clothes, and tried to think what else I could do to speed things up. I went to the window again.

Fifteen minutes later I heard the tractor. Great! They got it going. After that it only took ten minutes to chop the feed on the wagon.

We had all been delayed an hour or more. How quickly things happen. Our day off didn't go exactly as planned.

As our car hurried us to Green Lake, however, I thought about the swiftness and the power of these machines we work with every day. We had experienced a refresher course in respect for them, thankfully, without anyone getting hurt.

August, 1989

Dangerous Business

She looked a little younger than I, neatly groomed, sparkle in her eyes, ambition in her quick movements. As I watched her across the table at a wedding reception I surmised that she did not do any real work on the farm.

Then I noticed her hands with their oversized knuckles and some joints with nodules; probably from injury, arthritis, or over use. Tanned and full of strength, with blunt nails, these hands had experienced hard work. Later in conversation with her, I learned she had been a long time recovering from rotary cuff surgery, the kind baseball pitchers have. "Worst case we've ever had," the doctors told her.

"Guess it was from all the pitching, milking, and tractor driving," she said, a soft smile of satisfaction crossing her face. "Still bothers me. Missed the wagon tongue by an inch with the drawbar the other day. Thought I would just pull the wagon up—no way—the pain stopped me short."

I recalled looking down other tables at farm meetings and taking note of many hands with fingers shortened, mutilated, or entirely missing. I have watched men and women limp away from the table on replaced hips, and abused worn out knees that have experienced the surgeon's scalpel more than once. Everyone knows a farmer who has been killed on the job.

Farming is the most dangerous business in the United States, according to statistics that include the fatalities of children under age 14. If the kids are excluded from the calculations, farming is second only to mining in risk.

Sixty-seven farmers died in farm accidents in 1986 in Wisconsin, and 30 of them were over the age of 55. Officials are trying to figure out why it's higher and why more are older farmers. Is it more old machinery being used? Or more old farmers doing more of the work? Due to economic stress are farmers pushing harder to get more done in a day, increasing fatigue levels?

Believe me, it's not worth it.

I get uneasy when the men work in the rain or the dark, or when I know they are just too tired, or too much in a hurry.

We all know the rules. We don't need OSHA to hold our hand. What we do need is a slower pace, and to **THINK TWICE**:

* No, I am not faster than the gathering chain.
* When I'm working with lop-sided loads or on uneven terrain, the law of gravity always wins.
* The power take-off may be shut off, but even a slow moving knife can separate me from my finger.
* It's always the "tame" bull that does the killing.
* I may be strong, but the only way I'll stop a rolling wagon or a tractor, at even a snail speed, is over my dead body.
* Think "gas" around newly-filled silos and think "farmer's lung" when working with moldy or dusty crops.
* Chemicals are deadly.
* The power-take-off can undress me faster than a stripper— if I'm lucky. If I'm not lucky, I will be maimed or killed.

17

Once Upon A Farm

Henry was lucky. He once walked back from the field in only his J.C. Penney briefs. The post-hole digger wouldn't go down in our limestone, so he added his weight to it. The PTO grabbed his pant leg. Fortunately, the raggy old jeans tore easily. Only they were chewed up and destroyed by the machine, not his legs. Nowadays he's not too macho for goggles and masks when they are called for, or naive enough to think that his reflexes are faster than a machine's.

He hasn't worn his wedding ring for 30 years; ever since it and half of his finger held the weight of his body as he dangled from the rack of the old dump truck. I think he grew an inch that day, as he stretched out to his full height of 5 feet 7 inches and managed to touch the tips of his toes to the ground.

We thank God daily that major tragedy has not been part of our life. It can happen so fast, and stays with you forever.

September, 1987

A Need For Ben To Return

Two hundred years ago this past April he died. Ben Franklin possessed good logic: "Beware of little expenses; a small Leak will sink a great Ship." He also invented some simple and practical items, such as bifocals and lightning rods. It's time for him to come back. In this age of hormone tinkerers and computer freaks, the farm is ready for a few practical inventions.

For instance:

Robotical milkmaids that go down the line in the barn and automatically milk each cow. After all, the people doing it now feel like robots most of the time anyhow. If that's not possible, then a breed of cow with a kangaroo pouch-style holding tank on her side so she can hold her milk for two milkings. This would enable a milker to have a night off once in a while. (Christmas would be nice.)

"Instant Heal"— a product that is sprayed on teats that

18

have been cut, skinned, or mashed. The product doesn't have to restore lost flesh. Just repair the milk canal, kill the pain, and close up the wound a bit so a person can put the milker on it without being sent to the moon.

How about an electric fence (Ben liked electricity) that jolts cows but not humans? A lot of people who have worked on this farm would appreciate that. It would be nice to have a built-in alarm system that goes off in the house whenever a bovine body passes through the wire or gate. The alarm might be disturbing, but a cow bellering under your bedroom window at midnight isn't exactly a lullaby.

Another handy device would be a "Salesman Detector." Akin to a radar detector, it would sound as soon as one of them turn in at our mailbox; giving the men time to hide and myself time to create an escape diversion to use after opening the door.

It seems I'm always putting off lights that are left on. Our utility bill would nose-dive if someone could invent an affordable light that would go out when a body leaves the room or barn.

Since present day inventors like to deal in hormones, splitting embryos, and even cloning—you'd think they'd be able to come up with a simple pill for Mama Elsie, compelling her to calve during the day. Those 2:00 a.m. births are becoming too much for this aging mid-wife.

The men say they could use a welding rod that works at lower temperatures or else only welds metal and doesn't burn skin. A hammer that automatically detours thumbs would be helpful too.

I've often heard them express a desire for the gentleman who designed this XO#! piece of equipment to actually have to work with it; especially when slipping off poorly placed and wrong sized steps, or searching for oil filters hidden in inconvenient places. I'm sure someone could formulate a job description for engineers that would involve a little "on-the-job" seasoning.

Henry says the DNR should develop a breed of deer that only eats thistles and velvet leaf. They would have had a feast on our farm this year! (They did anyhow, but *not* on that diet.)

Once Upon A Farm

Dennis had only one request this summer: a mosquito repellent that *actually* works.

Everyone wishes for the weather service to devise some cloud seeds or wind tunnels or atmospheric humidity controls—anything—to return our weather system to some degree of normalcy.

Speaking of government services, it would be nice if the U.S. Dept. of Agriculture could concoct one survey that turned out to be accurate.

The farm shop would be easier on the laundry if a battery was designed that didn't spill out acid to eat holes in new jeans. (Why do they always wear the new jeans when changing batteries?)

Also appreciated would be grease that dissolves in cold water soap. That's not asking for too much, because we now have paints and even caulking that clean up with water.

It's getting close to year-end record keeping. Wouldn't it be nice to have a self-cleaning filing system? Just throw all the receipts, bills, instruction books, and literature into the file. Press a button, and whatever you would never need again would self-destruct. The remaining would arrange itself properly.

Where are you, Ben?

December, 1990

A Christmas Carol

Once upon a time it was the season of Christmas. Farmer Cratchit went to the barn as he did every day of the year. The Scrooge of Christmas was upon him. Today it was the barn cleaner chain that broke. It had moved only halfway around the barn before it snapped on the return corner outside.

Cratchit climbed the elevator in the cold wind to lift the cover off the gear box, so that he could force the chain ahead by hand. Then he picked the slack chain out of the manure and pieced it back together. His gloves became frozen wads of manure. He had to remove them to finish the

20

job. That night when he ate supper, the permeation of the scent reminded him of the morning's problem.

The chain should have been replaced last spring, but because of low milk prices there was no money. His creditors threatened to shut him off, so he made do with what he had.

When Cratchit got a little money ahead, he paid off some of Tim's medical bills. Everyone called his youngest son "Tiny Tim" because of his conspicuous height. At 6' 4" he towered over his father. The teenager had grown so fast that his cartilages tore easily and he often was on crutches. Cratchit couldn't afford $300 per month for health insurance.

Every day the farm press was filled with gloom and doom, saying that milk prices were going down again in '92. Mrs. Cratchit had taken a job in town to help out a little with the bills, so Bob Cratchit was left alone in the barn to struggle with broken parts, delays, and cows that sometimes chose not to enter their stanchions.

The kids weren't that much help. They were involved in all that sport stuff at school and only worked enough to get gas money and driving privileges for the old farm pick-up they begged to drive.

Even the weather seemed possessed by London-like gloom. First the biting cold and frozen ground came before Bob had a chance to finish plowing. Then it warmed up and rained every day. The fields became such a quagmire that he couldn't even spread manure. Bob worried about how the alfalfa roots would survive this drowning punishment. Then it snowed, melted, fogged, and snowed again. It was a Scrooge of a season.

Christmas Eve found Bob in the barn once more. Instead of taking part in the church celebration, he was here waiting for old Mary-belle to have her calf. She was his brood cow, the foundation of his herd. He hoped for yet another heifer, but she was ten days past due, and the possibility was slim.

After sweeping the manger hay for the cows to reach easily, his weary body collapsed on a bale and he dozed a little, dreaming of times past. Pleasant memories of times shared with his family on the farm filled his dreams . . . The joking and competitive stunts they took part in while picking stones in the spring; swimming and dunking each other in the pond after a sweaty day of haying; the trials of training Fair calves to the halter and then the pride and disappointments of ribbons won; teaching the kids to drive "straight stick" using the old pickup in the hay fields; and witnessing their ball games graduate from the farm lawn to the high school team. They were good kids and school was important. It seemed that for them, too, the day lacked enough hours.

Mary-belle forced with a cry of pain. Bob jumped off the bale, back to the present. The calf's head had appeared. Once past the ears, Mary-belle worked hard to complete the birth. Bob cleared the baby's nose, then grabbing the back legs, he pulled it around for the mother to lick. It was a heifer! From a good bull too! There is nothing like a birth to lift spirits. Once again awed by the miracle, Bob's spirits and hopes arose, as the new baby tugged at a bottle of colostrum.

His wife, home from the church service, came out to check on him. Together they walked to the house through fresh snow diamonds. It was beautiful in the country. Cratchit filled his lungs with a big sigh of fresh air.

Daughter Martha brought out a plate of his favorite nut cookies she had made. They poured homemade wine and opened presents. In a big shoe box labeled "Dad," Cratchit found a note from the boys—their gift—bold in black on white and unretractable, "We will do all the chores on Christmas morning."

It felt good to have his family around him. Cratchit envisioned that maybe the new year wouldn't be so bad. Perhaps the Scrooge-like times would have a change of heart.

Whatever—he still had his own health, the ability to work, and to determine what to do in the future even if it meant changing occupations.

Raising his glass, he toasted, "To a good life—and its simple pleasures. A Merry Christmas to us all, my Dears."

Tiny Tim, who shed his crutches that very morning, raised his glass last of all with a cheery, "God bless Us, Every One."

December, 1991

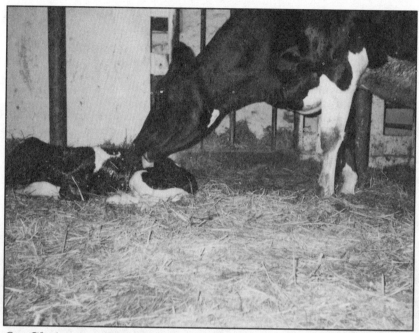

On Christmas Eve Mary-belle licks her newborn heifer calf.

In The Barn

A "TMR" Casserole

"What do you want for dinner?" I asked Henry after breakfast.

"I dunno. I'm not hungry now."

"A big help you are." We'd had plenty of chicken and ham at winter farm meetings lately. And my busy schedule had just about exhausted the "hamburger routine."

"I've got enough problems trying to figure out how to feed the cows," Henry answered back.

After thinking about it, I realized that his meal planning could be harder than mine. I try to balance our meals for protein, vitamins, minerals, and fiber, at the same time considering calories and texture. The cows demand the same. But to complicate matters, they have four stomachs! (Some teenage sons seem to be made the same way.)

Cows can eat fast, pulling huge amounts of feed and hay into the first stomach. Unlike the teenage son, they regurgitate what doesn't get chewed properly. The 120 lbs of saliva per day they secrete in the process is an important aid to digestion. When everything's working well they chew their cuds with that "contented look."

But things can go wrong. Feeds that are cut or ground too fine limit saliva production. Rations high in moisture and fermentation create a "sour" stomach, and have to be buffered with soda bicarbonate. The dairy industry is Arm & Hammer's biggest customer.

Consider that for much of the year the working cow is carrying her next calf while producing milk for the calf she just had, plus about 50 more pounds per day for humans to drink. Bossie needs lots of high quality feed in exact amounts to keep up a heavy milk flow rich in fat and protein. At the same time her body must be kept in shape—but yet not too fat because then she has calving and liver problems.

Once Upon A Farm

The farmer's challenge is producing or purchasing these feeds at a reasonable price. If your feed bill is bigger than your milk check the books don't come out well at the end of the month. Henry's weekly grocery list for our 50 bossies looks something like this:

175 bales of 18% protein hay
11,200 pounds corn silage
7800 pounds ground feed, consisting of corn, oats, tallow, whole soybeans, soybean and linseed meal, calcium, phosphorus, and salt.
Several big round bales and free-choice salt for "snacking" while they're outside (gotta keep 'em eating).

In addition he shops at the "Health Aid" counter for 100 pounds of minerals and vitamins that are hand fed to each cow to insure proper amounts of vitamin A, D, E, calcium, phosphorus, selenium, salt, and other trace elements.

All this has to be divided into as many feedings as possible to get the cow to eat her maximum and waste the minimum.

Henry sweeps the manger, urging his "girls" to eat more by putting the feed within easy reach.

With the shortage of qualified farm help, some farmers have turned to mixing a "cow casserole," using a machine that weighs and mixes the whole menu. TMR, or Total Mixed Ration, also allows them to substitute some cheaper forms of protein, such as feather meal, blood or meat and bone meal. Bossie can't pick around it. She has to eat the whole mixture. Cotton seed, distiller's grains, and corn gluten are also used.

Will a cow eat cardboard? No, not usually. But in TMR it can be mixed in for gross fiber, as can bakery wastes, and apple pumice. Other areas of the country make use of citrus pulp, crab shells, grape pulp, and banana plants.

Farmers near Hershey, Pennsylvania benefit from the candy company's "mistakes." Their cows dine on Kit Kats and Reese's Pieces, replacing more expensive energy feeds. It's one ingredient that doesn't have to be mixed in to get them to eat it. The cows love it!

A cow may eat some other things she should not. Found in cow's rumens have been money, nails, spikes, bolts, ball bearings, fork tines, and barb wire. If these puncture the stomach wall, Bossie can become very ill with an acute case of "hardware disease."

Well . . . I still don't know what to make for dinner. Maybe I'll try a casserole . . . I could slip in a few lima beans and call it the "TMR Casserole." Henry will be impressed.

March 1990

Why Did Tina Abort?

The two little babies lay in the gutter where their mother had deposited them. She had carried them only six months before going into labor early this morning.

About 18 inches long and weighing perhaps eight pounds each, the twin calves lay quietly in death, too small to survive outside the womb. Perfect little hooves appeared too big on legs that had no bone strength—legs that bent in any direction like wet noodles.

Once Upon A Farm

Both calves were bulls, easily identified by complete genitals. A bit of a tail was no bigger than a cat's tail. Perfectly formed tiny ears, eyes, and nose looked large on the bony head. Even though they were hairless, the markings were all there. Blotches of grey on soft pink skin outlined where at full-term would be black hair on white.

At first I thought they were identical, both having the same marks on neck and sides, but no—here one had an extra spot on his hip and the other a larger area of grey around the ears.

Now . . . why?

Why did Tina abort? Our first fear is always of disease. Abortion is a symptom of many serious, highly contagious cow diseases. Like a dark shadow, the fear of a Lepto or Johne's disease outbreak lurks in the backs of our minds. We read so much about it.

Henry phones the vet.

"Your vaccination program and management practices are good," he reassures us. "Don't worry, sometimes abortion just happens. Sometimes it's nature's way of ending a pregnancy that couldn't go full term."

Tina turned around to look at us, hay dangling out of both sides of her mouth as she chewed vigorously. Certainly nothing wrong with her appetite. She didn't appear sick at all. Three weeks ago she had pneumonia with temps up to 106 degrees, but now was fully recovered. Had the stress of the fever affected her pregnancy?

On the other hand, the first calf did come backward. Maybe it was just Mother Nature's way of solving a problem—knowing that the little cow could never carry it all off.

Anyhow, Tina had sealed her own death warrant. She had passed the calves easy enough, but not the afterbirth. It would no doubt cause infection in her uterus. This would have to be cleared up before we could even think about re-breeding. To keep her another year with no milk return just didn't make economic sense.

Tell that to my heart-strings. Tina was only 3½ years old. It wasn't that long ago that she herself was a frail little calf. Like so many of the "born small" calves, she seemed to have extra energy and appetite, growing rapidly, and soon becoming a pet. It all seemed so tragic.

But there were two young heifers in our feed lot that Tina had given us previously. She was still milking 50 pounds a day from that last calf, and should continue to do so for a while.

It isn't always easy, this business of cow-raising. One tries to look for good in the bad.

July, 1989

Udder Agony

Standing next to Honey Bea, I smelled something rotten. The two-year-old had calved a few days ago. Her high, tight udder bulged under her legs. In front of the right leg a smudge of blood was spread across the side of the udder. I put my hand under her leg and felt a piece of dangling skin. She had literally rubbed a hunk of skin off her udder!

This wasn't the first time we had this problem. I had tried a number of sprays, ointments, and drying powders. When our daughter worked in a nursing home she said, "Mom, why don't you try using Betadine? It works on bedsores."

So today I went to get my Betadine spritzer bottle. It's no miracle cure, but it does promote healing.

"You really trust her, don't you?" the herdsman said, watching me.

I was squatting behind Honey Bea, "Yeah, you know, some you can trust, some you can't." As I sprayed, she lifted her leg up and out as if to help me. She wouldn't think of kicking.

Now Lulu, the black heifer on the other side of the barn, was a different matter. She didn't appreciate anyone monkeying around under her legs!

I cleaned away the rotten debris on Honey Bea and sprayed the wound. This daily treatment would be continued for weeks. It wasn't easy to grow new skin in the absence of air, in a place that was dark, moist, and irritated anew every day as the udder filled with milk. Rather like treating a wound under your arm pit.

Once Upon A Farm

It seems we can't win. Years ago udders were long and hanging. The bag of a fresh, heavy milker almost scraped the ground. In this form, they were always dirty (especially after walking through mud) and often injured. So, udders were bred to stay high and tight with short teats—and now we have this new problem.

Not that we don't have any stepped on teats anymore either. I've never been able to figure out how a cow can do that to herself. I suppose it's a lot like stubbing your toe. By the time you feel the pain, it's too late to put your foot in a different place.

A stepped on teat can involve a little scraped skin off the side; or a "mash job" that damages the milk canal inside without a lot of outside damage; or a "mess" where the flesh is mangled, dripping blood and milk. Sometimes the teat dangles by a bit of skin. In some cases, fancy stitchery by a vet can repair it, but most often the wisest thing to do is "ship 'er out"—fast.

Recovery is a long, painful process for the dairyman and the cow. It usually involves milking the quarter by hand, or with a dilator, or a special cup. Any way you do it—it hurts—and the cow lets you know it. About the time a scab starts to form, it's milking time again and you open it up once more. She often gets mastitis in it, involving more treatment and expense.

"Cow bras" are the only answer for some older cows that become rather pendulous. The mesh bag holds the udder secure with a series of straps across her back and in front of her ribs.

As another preventive measure, we've started removing the dew claws on the inside of the back feet of newborn heifers; since some feel this may be the destructive instrument. Although sometimes it's a clumsy, long-legged neighbor that does a cow in.

Early spring seems the worst time of year for mammary destruction. The cows are more restless. I don't really know why. Maybe it's a little too warm in the barn and they get up more often to drink. Maybe they are stiff and joints are sore from being in the barn all winter, and they stretch out more. Some have difficulty getting up. Some folks think the

increasing daylight hours make cows more hyper. Maybe
they just sense that the fields are warming up with a change
in menu, and a change of scene. They're a little bored and
become restless.

Well, they're not alone. We're all a little restless and hyper
about the spring season.

April, 1989

The Dream Cow

"It's a girl—it's a girl!" I happily announced to Henry on
that October day two years ago. "Out of a top bull and our
best cow. Isn't that great?"

"Super."

I hurried to the house to heat a bottle of colostrum. Good
colostrum fed shortly after birth would give this precious
baby the start she needed for a long, productive life.

Cupping her chin in my hand, I eased the nipple into her
mouth. She sucked and tugged furiously. What would I call
her? A top cow should have a majestic name. Queen. That
would be good. She would be the queen of our herd.

A few days later I taught the perky calf to drink from the
pail. She was smart. I only had to lead her nose to the surface of the milk in the pail the first time. After that she
found it herself. She plunged her head to the depth of the
pail, milk coming up to her eyes. Discovering that it was
hard to breath under milk she soon learned to keep her
mouth on the surface—at least after the first moment of
excited eating time.

Queen was injected with vitamins, iron, and selenium.
She was vaccinated for lepto, IBR, haemophilus, and brucel-
losis. Horns and dew claws were removed so as not to injure
herdmates or herself when she eventually became a cow.

Queen was not only pretty to look at, she was fun to work
with. When I stuck my head in the pen, she would bound
over and lick my face or whatever part of me she could get
hold of.

The photos of her I sent in for registration portrayed a tall angular calf with typical Holstein markings. A white path down the center of her face was framed in black. Legs, tail, and body were white, with black garlanding her neck and spotting her rump, as well as saddling her middle. On her right side a diamond of white stood out in the field of black. It had to be a good sign.

As Queen matured and left the barn for the heifer lot, I could always pick her out by the long straight body and the distinctive mark of the diamond.

At 16 months of age Queen was bred to a "calving ease" bull that received good marks in the sire book. Queen's beauty blossomed even more as her body and udder filled out.

Calving time came at night (wouldn't you know). All went well. We took turns checking her progress, giving her enough labor time to make sure the cervix and vaginal muscles were pliant enough for the new little princess to pass.

But the little princess turned out to be a prince, ejected onto the straw in a rude awakening. We were a little disappointed, but Queen loved him anyhow and was soon on her feet caressing him with her tongue. Tired, and sure all was well, we went to bed.

First check in the morning showed Queen was working on her afterbirth. It's good she getting rid of that, I thought, then gasped. A large mass of whitish muscle laced with spider veins of blood protruded from Queen's enlarged vagina. She had not only passed the afterbirth, she never stopped forcing and now was passing her uterus. "Casting her withers" the old farmers called it.

The vet came and sterilized and shoved and sewed. But Queen made no effort to get up. He IV'd antibiotics, calcium, dextrose, electrolytes, and a few other things I was not familiar with. No response.

"I think something broke and she's bleeding internally," the vet said quietly. He administered another bottle of something—probably more for my sake than for the cow's, knowing I was not ready to give up on her. I slid an arm under the strong head stretched out on the straw. It was heavy. Her eyes were like marbles, devoid of life. The diamond on her side, which had been rising and falling with each breath, became motionless.

The next day as Queen's body was winched onto the truck a trickle of milk ran down the ramp, pressed from the bulging udder that held such promise. But the promise was ended. The dream was over.

"Hope springs eternal in the human breast," the poet says. Certainly in a farmer's breast. I have a new dream. Her name is Brandy. She's black and beautiful. I just know she'll be the queen of our herd!

November, 1989

Fighting The Bug

I set the pail of soured colostrum mixed with hot water in the rack of the calf crate. While the calf next door bumped her legs against the front of the crate and arched her neck to reach for her pail, this little calf just looked at me.

Cheryl (this little calf was named after a friend who was visiting the night she was born) put her mouth to the surface of the milk, then lifted her head slowly, the milk dripping off her chin back into the pail. Her ears were lowered instead of standing up perky like her neighbor, Sabel, who had already inhaled her milk. Cheryl stood quietly as if in shock. In a few minutes she lay down. The straw behind her was soaked with the yellowish, liquid bowel movement that every dairyman dreads as "scours," a killer.

I was not alarmed. The flu bug had been biting the cows. Winter dysentery is the intestinal disease which causes cows to only nibble at their feed, and have bowel movements that flood the platform behind them. We treat them with pastes and pills designed to stop the flow, heal the gut, and restore friendly stomach microorganisms. The vaccination program administered since birth is supposed to help them fight the bug. There are days you wonder who is winning the battle.

Highly contagious, the disease makes its way through the barn. You can track it by the splotches on the platform. A cow can seem to be over it, and then have a relapse. The bug thrives in the damp, quiet, warm air we've had so much of lately. Working the barn windows, doors, and fans, we try to keep dry, cool air moving in our old barn.

When the first calf got sick, I reached for the paste gun of lactobacillus, shoving a measure of it down her throat. The next day she was better. The others in the row of crates did not do as well. They would be good and then get worse again. Were they getting pneumonia?

The rectal thermometer showed only one had a fever, but we dosed them all with the antibiotics proven to work in our barn. Eventually they got better, but the bug lingered.

Now this calf, Cheryl, was passing blood. It seemed the bug was getting stronger. I didn't like to use antibiotics unless really necessary. I did not want to reduce any power they might have for Cheryl later in life, when she really needed them.

Falling back on some old remedies, I cracked an egg into an electrolyte solution. I had to keep up her energy and body fluids. Cheryl didn't want it. I poured it into a nipple bottle. Like any baby, she loved to suck and took to the nipple from which she had only recently been weaned. A few feedings of this and some lacto pills and Cheryl was bouncing in her crate again. I was winning!

In the meantime, Sabel next door got sick. I followed the same treatment. She was a very strong calf from an old cow that surely passed on to her a good supply of antibodies. Should be no problem.

Sabel did not seem very sick, but her bowels would not stop moving. Yet I could not believe it that morning when I walked into the barn, and saw the tail lying limp on the straw. The other calves were up and crying at the sound of my voice, but Sabel's body was flat in the straw of her crate. Her rear legs were drawn up, nose pushed down, eyes staring into the straw with a cloudy gaze. I knew without touching her that she was dead.

It had been years since I lost a calf and hadn't taken the killer seriously enough. All day I kept seeing the little body lying in the straw. "Why didn't I use antibiotics?" . . . "I should have known." . . . "Big dummy!" Having thoroughly kicked myself all day, I was glad to see Cheryl at night

swing her head over the edge of the crate, ears up, eyes
bright. She lunged for her milk.

You win some. You lose some. You learn some.

February, 1990

Under The Knife

The vet lifted his head and removed the stethoscope from
his ears. "I'll operate this afternoon. It's a D.A."

He had spent the past few minutes listening to the goings-
on inside of Jackie's stomach. Jackie had delivered her first
calf, a large bull, just two days before. Since then she had
lost all interest in food, only nibbling at hay now and then.
Having no fever, and passing only a small amount of
manure, we suspected this to be the problem.

D.A. stands for displaced abomasum, which a farmer may
refer to as a "twisted gut." It really hasn't twisted, only
moved from its normal position.

That afternoon when the familiar truck with the big medical cabinet in its bed rolled into the yard, I went out to
watch. My contribution to the procedure was to tie the dog,
Dixie.

Dr. Bill didn't need the lively pup messing around with his
equipment. Bill's "black bag" was a large stainless steel kit
equipped with an assortment of surgical instruments, rolls
of sutures, and various needles. He balanced it across large
plastic pails to keep it off the barn floor.

The operating arena was the cow's own stanchion, complete with over-head cobwebs. Bootsy, most inquisitive of
the barn cats, took up a watchful position nearby.

"Is this the way you thought it would be when you were in
vet school?" I asked.

"Let's just say that there's a certain art to keeping your
surgery sterile in a relatively dirty environment,"
he answered kindly.

I thought it an understatement.

Dr. Bill's first step was to secure the cow's head with a
nose lead. Then he positioned Dennis, the herdsman, at her

tail to keep her from moving around too much. Jackie would have her surgery standing up, fully awake!

"She's more comfortable that way and her rumen will keep working," explained Bill while shaving and sterilizing the area of skin just in front of her right flank. Then he injected Lidocaine throughout the area. "It's what your dentist uses when he freezes your mouth, only this is about twice as strong."

I felt a little better knowing that Jackie wasn't going to feel anything of what was to follow. Dr. Bill prepared himself by stripping to his undershirt in the 50 degree barn, and donning sterile gloves. He lifted a tray of instruments from chemically sterile solution and set them to drain on the opened lid of his surgical case.

Before I knew it his deft movements had opened an eight inch incision through the skin and three muscle layers, into the abdominal cavity. "There is a lot of gas trapped in there. That abomasum is twice the size it should be. I'll have to bring it back down to size before we can put it back where it belongs." His hand disappeared into her side as he pushed a needle attached to a rubber hose into the distended stomach.

After he was satisfied with those results, he started pulling on the organ, hand over hand. "See that? It's called a pig's ear." He held a thick ruffled portion. "That's a landmark. It means we're in the right place, working on the right part, the fourth compartment. They say a cow has four stomachs. Really it's only one stomach with four compartments."

The maneuvering continued. "I want to make sure it's all where it belongs." He clamped some tongs onto part of the stomach. "Here, Dennis, hold this right here. I'll tack it in place with two big stitches, so this problem can't repeat itself."

The doctor proceeded to sew up the two inner muscle walls. Just before closing he squirted in a syringe full of penicillin to prevent possible infection. Another layer of stitches closed the outer muscle wall, and a third seam closed the skin. He was quite a seamstress with his long scissor-like instrument that held a curved needle with which he pulled the chronic gut. "It's referred to as 'cat gut' but it usually comes from sheep."

"That should make you happy, Bootsy," I said to the cat
still perched on a nearby bale, her eyes intent on the flicker-
ing needle. Bill had a fancy name for his neat handiwork,
but to me it looked like a buttonhole stitch.

Jackie showed no sign of discomfort except for a few
flinches when the final stitches were put in. Bill concluded,
"She's a little ketotic because she hasn't been eating. She's
started to burn her own body fat. We'll I.V. some dextrose.
Keep her on penicillin for a few days."

The whole procedure was neatly done in about an hour.
There was about a cupful of blood in the straw underneath
Jackie; not at all the gory mess I had anticipated.

"Why did this happen to her, Doc?" Dennis asked.

"Abdominal stress, usually related to calving. Can be
caused by a lot of things: big calves, cows with big bellies,
too finely chopped silage, lack of exercise, poor feet. We
notice it's more dominant in some bull lines. So are cysts
and a few other problems. I wish they would stop breeding
and pushing for production. We have enough milk. How
about trying to breed a healthy cow?"

I agreed wholeheartedly. I'm sure Jackie did too.

March, 1988

Babies In The Cold

I laid my face against the head of the new-born calf. The
silky hair was too new to even have a barn smell. I only
smelled the warmth of its body edged with the scent of
summer sun still clinging to the wheat straw that formed its
bed. A moist nose nuzzled my cheek, searching for
nourishment.

It was a small-sized calf, but chubby. My first inclination
was to take the teddy-bear-like animal into the house and
cuddle it on the kitchen floor, while the sub-zero wind
howled outside. But I knew the little critter had to get used
to the cold, and the sooner the better.

His mom was hovering over us and licking my shoulder

Once Upon A Farm

as if the calf and I were one. The calf sucked the 2½ quarts of colostrum out of the big nippled bottle in short order, not taking a moment to rest and continuing to pull on the nipple until I heard the slurping sound of sucking air.

I could have let him find his own way to his mother's swollen teats; but this way I knew he'd get milk soon and get enough, most critical to developing his immune system. That doesn't always happen when you leave them to their own bumbling efforts. Pneumonia is a big killer of calves.

Not that the mother wasn't trying. She lowered her head and chased a friendly cat out of the pen. No strange thing was going to come near her precious baby! But the breath she exhaled, along with the breath of the 49 other cows, was moist and laden with germs, the worst thing for a vulnerable new-born. He would be much better off breathing the cold air of the calf building, or better yet—put right outside!

That's the reason you see little round or oblong hutches gathered on the lee side of many dairy barns. But isn't that *too* cold? Don't you have to feed them more to maintain the extra energy they burn up just keeping warm?

To get the answers firsthand, I visited Kelly and Keri while they did their nightly calf feeding chores on the Kaufman farm east of Berlin. The slim girls, 10 and 13, quickly carried pails of waste milk from the milk house to fiberglass igloo-like huts.

The calves inside saw them coming, and banged their legs against the pail racks as they pressed forward in eager anticipation. Underneath the calves was a thick bed of dry straw. The girls poured and the strong calves, sporting coats of thick fur, drank eagerly. Kari put a bottle in a rack for a two-day-old baby and guided the calf's nose over to it.

"Hurry up!" Kari said, her thin shoulders scrunched up. "It's cold out here!"

"We feed twice as much milk in winter as in summer," said Kelly, a proud smile on her face as she poured more milk. "They need more to keep warm."

Next to its milk pail each calf had a pail of starter feed. Dad Wayne joined us to explain that they stay on the starter longer than required to ensure adequate nutrition in the cold.

38

"It's worth the extra expense to have healthy calves," added his wife, Jo Ann.

"Once in a while an ear might get frosted a bit," said Wayne. "But that don't hurt 'em. On the whole they do a lot better in the cold."

Back home, my precious new baby was carried off to the cold ventilated barn. Once out of his mother's sight, she would not miss him and would go about the business of eating and drinking and producing milk.

From now on I was his mother and he would depend on me for daily food and attention, soon rising at the sound of my voice. He'll grow his own warm coat and adapt to his environment, doing better that way than if I keep him too warm with no fresh air.

Not that different from raising kids, I mused. Parents can't always cover them with smothering warmth. They, too, have to learn to grow and adapt.

February, 1989

An Empty Stanchion

"You mean you want to bring her in right now?" I asked with one hand browning hamburger for chili, the other creaming butter for cookies. (Cold weather always puts me in a cooking mood.)

"Yeah, right now, why not?" Henry said impatiently. "I was just thinking of how cold it is. There's no sense having that dry cow outside, when a stall is empty."

Even if it was mid-morning, New Year's Day, he couldn't relax and had been pacing all morning. The empty stall he was referring to belonged to Wilma, who now lay in the maternity pen. Wilma was dying. His decision to fill her stall meant he had given up hope for her.

"Okay, I'll be right there," I said quickly and shut off the burner. I put on my insulated vest and jacket; then tied on two cotton scarves, one across my forehead, the other under my chin. My garb was not much for looks, but was good protection against the Siberia-like outdoors.

Once Upon A Farm

The sun was bright and cheery, but the wind was biting with the thermometer at three degrees. Bambi, the dry cow who had been exiled to the heifer lot, was standing alone on the south side of the barn where she was protected from the cold. Even so she didn't look very happy. Her hair coat had thickened as temperatures dropped, but with her tail between her legs, her back hunched and head lowered, she looked cold. She would be the last dry cow put out until warmer times in March. We've found it just doesn't pay. Adjusting to the extremes of sub-zero and then coming into the warm barn seem to take more out of their production capabilities than one gains by the practice of keeping a few extra milking cows.

First we moved the young cow that was in Bambi's stall over to Wilma's, because we always let the old girls have their own place back. The young ones get moved around until a permanent place is available for them.

It didn't take long for Bambi to find the open door. Her long legs nimbly scampered up the steps. It was because of those long legs that I had given her the name of a deer. She scrambled to her usual stanchion with eagerness. Her actions seemed to say, "You mean I can come in? It's too good to be true, but I'll take it—fast."

We went to the pen and looked at Wilma. Her stomach looked bloated in spite of the fact that she hadn't eaten a thing for three days. Her body muscles seemed to have lost all tone. Putting my hand on the seven-year-old, 1500 pound body, her skin felt cold and clammy. Her temp was 95 degrees, six degrees below normal. Each exhale of air from her lungs was accompanied by stench and a low guttural groan. Her look was of complete resignation.

It was baffling. Wilma had gone two weeks past her due date, when finally on Christmas morning she easily gave birth to a huge baby. "Must weigh 120 pounds," Dennis said, staggering under the squirming weight as he carried the calf to a crate. We were delighted it was a heifer in spite of its late arrival.

"Mom, why don't you name her Joy?" our holiday-visiting daughter suggested.

Wilma had milk fever that evening and again the next

morning. Each time she responded with miracle-like reaction to the intravenous calcium. The next day she was fine, gave lots of milk, and was let out for exercise. The following afternoon she quit eating and her body turned cold. More calcium brought warmth for only half an hour.

"Must be something else wrong. Something must have broken inside," Henry mused. The vet's probing hands, and mind, and stethoscope brought no answers. Wilma submitted herself to us as we forced electrolytes, lactobacillus, and fluids down her throat, and antibiotics into her uterus and veins. She did not respond. After giving her free room and board the last two months while she was dry, now we were going to lose both the anticipated milk and her meat.

Tomorrow the ominous-looking, black stock truck would turn in our yard. With a rifle bullet between her eyes, Wilma would be put out of her misery. The grand body that had given us three fine daughters and a lifetime production of 115,000 pounds of milk, would be winched from the barn with a cable around her neck—not what she deserved and not what I wanted to see. The truck driver would hand Henry $7.00 for the magnificent beast.

That's the way it is. It happens.

Before we left the barn we looked at the young cow we had moved to Wilma's stall. It happened to be her own daughter, Gabriel (also born at Christmas). A big black beauty like her mother, she held a lot of promise. I went to Joy, at one week old already an orphan—she would never know. Getting up quickly, she nuzzled my hand. So strong and lively, eagerly nibbling at her calf starter, she indeed promised "joy."

We went back to the house. Henry felt a little better. An empty stanchion is so depressing. Settling in his chair, he turned on the bowl games. I turned the burner back on under the chili and got out a bag of chocolate chips for the cookies.

January, 1988

Classified "Excellent"

"I guess you know who I am," said the stout woman, turning to shake my hand. "You received a letter explaining this procedure?" she questioned.

Yes, we had been notified of the classification of our 30 purebreds and 20 identified grades. Today was the day of their "beauty contest" and I was as a nervous mother, hoping her children looked their best while reciting their Christmas piece.

As I followed the classifier, walking behind the cows, admonishments raced through my mind. "Charity, don't let your back sag now." "Stand up straight, Ani." "Keep your head up, Princess, you look much taller that way."

The jean-clad woman, appearing to be in her thirties, eyeballed each animal from all angles. It was soon obvious that she knew cows, and not much was going to escape her scrutiny. Maybe it was because she was a woman doing a job most often performed by men that she was very serious, and all business as her pencil began marking numbers on the worksheet.

Duchess got a high mark for stature. She was tall, her backline level with my nose when I stood next to her. I thought she was a beauty. Being strong, but not fat, my hopes went up for a high score. However, her legs were her undoing. Her rear legs hocked in and there was not enough angle to her foot, meaning her weight was not carried correctly. Guess I had never looked at her that way. I was disappointed.

The shiny black body of Party (my birthday present three years ago) was next in line. I hoped the layer of fat across her shoulders and filling out her rump would go unnoticed. No such luck. "Dairy Form" was marked only fair. No matter, I still liked her.

At the end of the row, Chantilly swung her broad head around in the tie stall, looking at us as if to say, "Hi, what do you want?"

The classifier stood behind her. In a cool, no-nonsense way she was filling in the blanks with good numbers for form, rump, and teat placement. At the end of the line she wrote two E's and the number 90. E meant "Excellent" and Chantilly was our first cow ever to earn this rating.

My hopes were fulfilled! It was like your kid being named "student of the year." After 35 years of milking and breeding cows—a reason for celebration.

The object of all this is to grade cows and breed them to improve their faults. Bulls are also graded and you match weaknesses with strengths. Sounds simple. In no time at all we should all have "super" cows. Not so.

We've bred a cow with bad legs to a bull screened to improve that trait—but he carried a recessive gene of short stature. The calf born of that mating was small with bad legs! The good genes didn't come through.

It's that way with people too. Ideally, I should have inherited Aunt Ruth's beauty, Mom's strength, and Pa's disposition. The good genes didn't come through. I'll never make "excellent."

In spite of their faults, some of our worst looking cows are our best, most dependable milkers. Somehow, what I like about them obscures their bad points.

The goodness of some people obscures their "bad genes."

Striving for perfect cows makes farming challenging, while the imperfections of the human race keep life interesting.

What would we talk about if everyone classified "excellent"?

December, 1988

Belle's Christmas Wish List

"All I want for Christmas is for the cows to milk themselves—just once," the young farmer said.

Most farmers would agree that would be a nice Christmas present. It would give them free time to watch their kids in the church program; since farmers have become such a minority, churches no longer schedule events with cows or farmers in mind. There might even be time to travel to Grandma's for a family meal and celebration, without either arriving late or leaving early because of chores.

I can think of a lot of other things on a farmer's wish list, but what would a cow want for Christmas? I was scratching Belle's neck the other day and she whispered in my ear.

Once Upon A Farm

This is what she said:

"To get through a year without being pregnant, that's what I'd ask for. (Some of our cows are trying hard for that wish.)

"Then I wish my drinking cup was cleaned each day. How'd you like to have your water strained through hay stems and silage slime?

"Next I wish for a pail of hot water for the milker cups to be dipped into. You see, I'm the first cow milked and I'd sure appreciate the teat cups warmed up before they're slapped on. That cold, stiff rubber sends chills up my spine. (Belle shivered a bit when she said that.)

"I wish my bed could be made a little better, a little more often. Oh, I know some fresh straw gets shaken over the top every day, but I really don't like the smell of that crud packed in the corners. I appreciate the rubber mat, but once in a while I'd like a fresh 'mattress pad.'

"Fairness—that's what I'd like for Christmas. Elsie, the cow next to me, gets twice as much grain as I do, and she's not even as big as I am. What's more she doesn't even eat it all! When I get down on my front knees and stretch out my neck and tongue to take a little, someone slaps me on the back. That's gratitude for you, when I'm just trying to keep good feed from going to waste. I always clear my own plate 'lickin' clean.' It's just not fair.

"Shots, I hate 'em. I wish Henry would get some new sharp needles for Christmas. It might be a little less painful. You know, sometimes I think he delights in sticking me with that needle. He does it when I don't even feel sick!

"I wish I could come and go as I pleased. When I want to stay in they make me go out, and when I want to stay out they make me come in. Take that day it was snowin' and blowin' so hard. I didn't see any reason for exercise, but then Dennis hollers, 'C'mon girls, let's go, let's go—out!' And then the day the sun was shining so nice, I would have been content to chew on the old hay in the feeder and lie against it in the sun, but then Dennis says, 'C'mon girls, get in there.' It's enough to make a 'holy cow' sacrilegious.

"I wish I would get some respect. Cold as it is, Dennis opens that hay chute right above me. Frigid air blows right down my neck. Then a prickly bale bounces on my head. I wish he would use the other chute and carry all the bales across the barn. Show an old girl a little respect.

"A new hair-do and a manicure would be a nice Christmas present. All that dust from the bale chopper and musty hay settles around my tailbone. The lice love it. Itching nearly drives me crazy some days. And my one front toe nail is getting so long that it's curving into the other one. Makes it painful to walk. A hoof-trim and a good going over with the cow-vacuum or curry comb would feel so good . . . why, I probably wouldn't hit anyone with my tail for a whole year."

Well, farming friends, I can't do much about the cows milking themselves at Christmas. But if you can make some of your Belle's comfort wishes come true, she just might make you a present of a little more milk. A Contented and a Blessed Christmas to you all.

December, 1989

That First Christmas Happened On A Farm

After coming home from choir practice, I changed into my barn clothes and went out to check a cow due to calve.

The night was quiet. The sky filled with bright points of stars that seemed especially clear and close to me tonight. Strains from the song, "O Holy Night," kept running through my head.

Inside the barn, Spritz (herself born at Christmas) sprawled flat in the maternity pen, udder bulging from under her leg. With her head stretched out in the straw, I couldn't tell if she was sleeping, or in early stages of labor. Deciding to wait a while and find out, I sat on a bale of straw, watching and listening.

A single bulb gave dim light to the birthing area. From the dark depths of the long barn came the quiet sounds of animals at rest: the crunching sounds of a few slow eaters still chewing on hay with rhythmic motion; the heavy breathing of others sound asleep, their heads resting in the

45

manger. Most were quietly rotating their jaws on cuds. From far down the row came a low, hum-like groan, repeating every few minutes. Probably a very pregnant old girl, too uncomfortable to lie and too tired to get up. I could relate.

The refrain of music came back through my head again, and I thought of the barn at Bethlehem. Though surely different in structure, the sounds and smells were probably much the same: the earthy smell of fresh manure; the herb-like essence of fresh-cured straw and hay; and the sounds of animals moving and eating.

I couldn't imagine myself giving birth in a barn. Yet— why not? It was private and warm. The cave that was used as a stable by local herdsmen in Bethlehem's hillside, was no doubt as clean as any other place during the crowded time of census registration.

I could see Joseph making a bed with the straw given him by the farmer. At one side of the rough rock wall a manger was hollowed out of stone. He filled it with straw for the expected baby's cradle.

Mary had brought with her the long strips of linen with which to bind the child's limbs, so he would grow straight and strong. When her labor began, Joseph found a midwife in the nearby town.

The donkeys and oxen had run out of the cave when the unfamiliar couple made their entrance. But as the morning light edged the hills, hunger drew the animals back to the scent of the dried grass piled inside. They edged to the door, ears bent forward, listening to the strange sounds within.

The manger where they usually ate now smelled of olive oil, salt, and of a strange body. Something wonderful had happened in their barn!

I was brought back to the reality of our own barn by the loud rush of escaping breath from Spritz's nostrils. With much effort the heavy cow lurched to her feet. Ambling over to the manger, she pulled up a big mouthful of thick-stemmed hay.

No great event was happening in our barn tonight. Yet, I felt honored that God chose a humble work place such as ours to send his son for that very first Christmas.

Maybe that's the reason most farmers feel a special closeness to God.

December, 1988

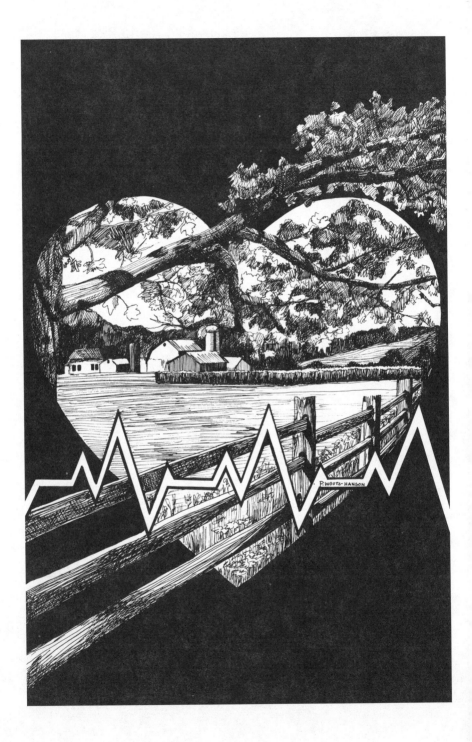

Rural Rhythms

February Blues

Even the dog is bored.

Dixie, our lab pup, puts her front feet up on the barn door. Bounding outside she runs through the snow, circles back and pounces on a stray corn husk caught in a drift.

I've finished hauling water to the calves in their frigid winter quarters. The chores are done one more time. My fingertips start to hurt as the cold stops the blood from circulating.

My patience is short. "Dixie, you dummy. You can't stay out all night . . . I'm in no mood for games . . . Get your tail in here!"

She takes one look at the open door and runs the other way. Tired of chasing cats and stealing gloves, she has discovered exciting scents and scenes outside. She doesn't want to be confined any longer. I end up grabbing her by the collar and dragging her to the barn.

It's the same old thing for a lot of us: known as "February Blues." Go to work in the dark. Return in the dark. Feed the animals and clean up after them. Feed the family and clean up after them. The daily routines are getting boring.

Depression sets in and is expressed by people being ornery and really on edge. As sure as you plan an exciting event, bad weather is bound to spoil it.

Not that there isn't anything to do. There are farm training and sales meetings to attend, including everything from picking the right bulls to learning about the new herbicides. But after rushing around in the cold to finish chores and get there in time, the meetings often become more of a challenge to the body to stay awake than for the mind to learn.

Then there is cleaning. Any "spring" housecleaning on the farm has to be done in winter when there is more time. The house has plenty of job opportunities for me. I must

Once Upon A Farm

have the most active spiders in the county! There are over-flowing drawers and closets that I can't ignore much longer.

If that doesn't appeal to me, there's always the barn. Talk about cobwebs! The outsides of the pipeline and airline need washing often, and build-ups need to be scraped from floors.

The milkhouse demands hours of scrubbing walls and cabinets. Butterfat residue and milkstone need an acid soak and elbow grease before they will depart from sinks and washtanks. Stainless steel only looks clean when it is clean.

A trip to the implement store for pipeline soap provides diversion when I tire of cleaning. It's the highlight of my day. What do I see? Jeff is cleaning too. Counting all those lousy little nuts and bolts, dusting under them, and then putting them back. What a bore compared to a few months hence, when his skill will be in demand to get the exact part needed as fast as possible so the farmer's crop can go in.

Recently I read of a farmer having trouble with tail-biting among his pigs. (Immediately I related it to some people I know.) He decided that part of the problem was confinement and boredom, so he put a bowling ball in their pen. It created a diversion. Maybe that's the answer.

Part of the problem is the colors of winter. Shades of gray, cold blues, bleak blacks, and wimpy (dirty snow) whites are not much to get excited about.

One morning I look out our south bow window and see bright bits of red flashing in the lilac bush. It's a pair of cardinals at the feeder! That spot of color perks me up. God always provides a little lift when we need it.

My eyesight falls to the pile of seed catalogs waiting for my attention. The scarlet photo of the All-American Rose beckons to me. I pick up the books and settle in the rocker by the window. Oh, that sun *IS* getting warmer. On another cover is a Missouri Primrose. They did well last year with their continuous lemon-yellow blooms. I'll order some more. I have to be careful though. My February-ordering-eyes are usually bigger than my May-planting-abilities. It would be fun to start a Kiwi vine though . . . and maybe some sugar peas. I feel better already.

February, 1988

50

What's In A Name

The calf was white, all white. Ink spots on the tips of her ears and black freckles on a tiny pink nose were the only markings.

Her "first-time-mother" didn't do much licking to clean off the birth membranes. So after I fed her heated colostrum from our freezer, I rubbed her down with a gunny sack. She still looked a bit pathetic, her skinny body shivering as she struggled to keep her balance on wobbly legs. Watching her I wondered, what will I name this one?

Next morning she was stronger and could stand easily. Her hair, now dry, was soft and thick as a plush stuffed toy. Hopefully she would be a good cow like her grandmother, Lady Diana, born on the day of that royal wedding. The mother, Leia, was a daughter of the bull, "Star Wars," so she was labeled with a name from that movie. Such is the method of my madness in naming my charges.

For instance, Grace was born on the day our congregation voted to build a new church, and Bucky arrived on the first day of deer hunting. Some names reflect weather conditions at the time of birth such as Blizzard, Twilight, and Snowflake.

Over the years births have hit most of the holidays, inspiring names like Noel and Eve, Schnappsie, Love and Cupid, Bunny, Lambie, and Liberty. Twins born at Easter were Jelly and Beany. The set arriving on Christmas day were tagged Holly and Ivy.

Naturally, some names give clue to the color of the animal like Salty, Frosty, Blondie, Spot, and Licorice. Teddy Bear, Penguin, and Panda looked just like their namesakes.

The disposition of the animal makes some names a must, such as Dynamite, Goofus, Devil, Sparky, Bimbo, Lightening, Angel Puss, Lovey, and Pal.

Other names are witness to physical attributes. Observe Pee-Wee, Minnie, Tina, Twiggy, and Wobbles. On the other end of the scale are Moosie, Lurch, Amazon, Droopy, and Dandee.

Most of our friends and family will find their names in our

Once Upon A Farm

herd records. Yes, we even had a Henrietta!

But what about this beautiful white daughter of Leia, sired by Ned Boy?

Henry gave me the answer with his question, "Can we name that white calf Julia?" He usually had little interest in the naming process, but I knew what he was thinking. He was a teenager when his parents, Julia and Henry Sr., started milking cows and went to auctions looking for animals. As city transplants, they didn't know anything about pedigrees or type, and couldn't afford purebreds.

"Look at the pretty white calf," Julia once said, as she watched it kicking its heels while waiting to be sold. She always favored the white ones. Her nick-name for all little ones she loved (kids or animals) was "Cookie." To please her, Henry's dad bought the calf and "Cookie" came home with Julia.

Over the years that calf's descendants became the back-bone of our herd. Following the lineage, I have named some of them Chips, Ginger, Pfeffer (nusse), Spritz, and Oreo. They weren't all white, but they were all hard working animals.

It was in tribute to his mother, and the memories of her and her love of the little white calf, that Henry wanted the name "Julia" in the purebred records.

What's in a name? A great many things. Especially people surnames. During his freshman year, a plaque hung above our son's desk in his college dorm. It was inscribed with these words:

You got it from your father, it was all he had to give.

So it's yours to use and cherish, for as long as you may live.

If you lose the watch he gave you, it can always be replaced.

But a black mark on your name, son, can never be erased.

It was clean the day you took it, and a worthy name to bear.

When he got it from his father, there was no dishonor there.

So make sure you guard it wisely, after all is said and done.

*You'll be glad the name is spotless, when you give it to
your son.*

January, 1988

Life Is Fragile

I darted through the pouring rain back to the house,
wondering what to do. It was 1:30 a.m. "Matilda" was in the
maternity pen and six days overdue.

"Her water is broke, but she isn't starting any forceful
contractions yet," I reported to my sleeping husband.
"Should we get up again?"

"She's a big cow, she should have it okay by herself. At
least she can wait four hours until we're out there, "Henry
said without even opening his eyes.

So I went into an uneasy sleep. The bull she was bred to
had a lot of type but, we were discovering, a lot of size also.
Of the four calves we had from him, three were bulls weighing over 100 pounds.

I was fully awake again at 5:30 a.m. as the phone rang
next to our bed. Henry was up and out in the barn.

"We need your help." I heard his urgent voice, "It's coming backwards."

There was no time to wait for the vet. Matilda was
exhausted. She was all stretched out flat on her side, her
head flat on the floor, white foam spilling from the sides of
her mouth. Her distorted stomach rose and fell as she
breathed rapidly, but she was too tired to force anymore.
She had my total empathy.

One hind leg of the calf had made it through the birth
canal. Henry had the disinfected water and the lubricant.
He had the chain on the one leg, his arm deep inside the cow
searching for the other leg. I positioned the calf jack on the
cow's body and lubricated her vagina, as he secured the
chains and applied gentle pressure.

Matilda started working once more. Timing their efforts
with hers, Henry and Dennis inched the big legs out. Once
the hips popped out they jacked quickly so the calf wouldn't

drown, knowing that as soon as its cord broke it would try to breathe. If its head was in fluids, that's what it would inhale.

It was another very large bull. Quickly Henry and the hired man hoisted his back legs to the top of a pen post. They hung him upside down so the fluids could drain out. The calf was motionless—its eyes fixed.

"He's gone," Henry mumbled as he slapped the rib cage trying to get things going. Then he felt one heartbeat—then a few more erratic throbs. I picked up a clean straw and jammed it hard into the calf's nostril. It jerked and snorted, blood and water coming out of its mouth.

After a bit they laid him in the straw. He could not lift his head, only stretched it out and cried in the most pitiful thin bawl. Matilda was on her feet, licking and nuzzling and talking to him in soft little moos of contentment. The calf kept on crying.

This was not usual. Henry phoned the vet. "What is wrong? Is there anything else we can do?"

The vet's reply came in calm steady words, "A blood vessel in the lungs may have broken from the ribs being jammed the wrong way during a backwards birth. Some ribs may even be broken. It's not major damage. He should be all right."

We built a pen of straw bales, with deep bedding. I covered the limp wet body with gunny sacks and an old rug. He finally stopped crying. Although he wanted to suck, he choked on the colostrum I offered from the calf bottle. Still too much mucus on his throat. He needed time and rest.

By that afternoon he could hold his head and suck and swallow. The following morning he was on his feet by himself. Once again we had witnessed the miracle and fragility of life.

We knew our problems were not over, however. It was almost a sure thing that Matilda would not pass her afterbirth, because of the stress of her difficult calving. Her uterus would have to be packed and treated with antibiotics more than once. Even then we would probably have problems getting her bred back in 60 days. We wouldn't be using semen from that bull anymore. It wasn't worth the risk.

The risk turned out even greater, when a few days later Matilda started hemorrhaging. The men and the vet worked for three hours giving her blood-clotting drugs, transfusions from other cows in our herd, and even packing her uterus with a bed sheet. She simply put her head down into the straw and died.

It is just one of those freaky things you are supposed to expect and absorb. But it's hard.

That same day our grown daughter had not returned from a trip when expected. When she phoned to say she was all right, I quickly breathed a prayer of thanks that it was only a cow that died.

June, 1987

It's Time To Catch Your Breath

"So what are you doing now that the second crop hay is in?" my Winneconne cousin asked.

I caught my breath and stopped to think for a minute. There was no big important job underway, just oodles of little ones calling for attention.

There are calves that need dehorning, and herd records and vaccinations that need updating. The back door is screaming for paint, and four inches of frost on the sides of the freezer take some blame for our rising electric bill.

It's time to trim the shrubs and fight the spiders for clear window vision. Aunt Katie needs to be invited out for a few days, and my brother is waiting for our visit in Illinois. It's time for family reunions and my high school reunion (again!). It's time to can green beans and to savor the taste of fresh cucumber salad and that first tomato!

For the men it's time to fix right the tractors and machinery that have been "band-aided" through the rush of planting and haying. The old John Deere needs a new generator. The haybine sickle needs sharpening. The source of an oil leak in the Bobcat must be found. The grease gun begs for action. Henry spends a half day stemming the tide of a dripping-turned-streaming drinking cup in my calf barn.

Once Upon A Farm

Now's the time to repair that fence, nail up those boards, and hang that gate. It's time to clean the steer yard and heifer pens. The tree branches that tug at the house rain gutters every time the wind blows need to be trimmed, as well as the now-dead branches that didn't survive the June slush storm.

It's also Fair Time. Many farm kids are scrubbing and polishing all kinds of things from calves to hand-made projects such as wooden lamps and dirndl skirts. Parents are prompting and threatening and adjusting chore hour schedules. They share fully in each pink ribbon as well as the blue. Winnebago County Fair opens for the first time at its new location on August 15. Dennis spent a day there along with other area farmers, volunteering their time and labor so that, for the young people, "the show can go on." Donations from the farm sector was the only way the county would put up a milk house.

It might just be time to let even the little jobs go and spend a day at the park or the beach with the kids. Or at least take time to appreciate the good season we're having. The rain did come this year. (Every day for a while even when we didn't want it!) The corn is trying hard to make up for time lost during the cold wet spring. While drought continues in parts of the south, floods have swamped parts of Iowa and Wisconsin, and hail stones pelleted many crops, here in the Berlin area we have been spared. The apples are getting fat, and the gold of grain fields against the dark green of corn are summer's most splendid colors. Take time to say a prayer.

All too soon the race will be on again: shopping for school clothes; combining and baling straw; third crop haying; corn harvest and the work that follows takes us right up to Christmas.

Sit down and catch your breath. Watch a bluebird, or a barn swallow caring for its young—the butterflies' busy flight, white and yellow against the green alfalfa—the wild tiger lilies that burst with new brightness each day. Take in the beauty of a tree as her green garments rustle in a summer breeze. Watch the sun go down, or come up, either way full of beauty and inspiration.

Appreciate your kids' delight as they play in a sprinkler or pool, the wag of your dog's tail, the touch of your spouse's hand on your cheek as you doze in your recliner. Preserve these "summer" memories for the "cold days" sure to follow.

The most important job you have this summer may be a multitude of little ones, or it may be to take time and catch your breath. God allows each of us only so many.

August, 1990

Fire Doesn't Consume Everything

The entry in my old journal is dated August 3, 1973 as follows:

After dinner Henry went out to go combining. Hearing sirens, he looked around and saw smoke over the hill. We jumped into the car and drove up to the highway.

"Arnie Nummerdor's barn!" Henry said, his voice strained with disbelief.

It was obviously already a total loss and the fire trucks had just gotten there. We didn't want to get in anyone's way, but wanted to offer barn space to the now-homeless cattle rushing out to the marsh pasture. All were saved except one sick calf and a cow that Dick (Arnie's son) had left in the barn that day because he just found out she sucked others.

Dick had just finished combining and baling straw and second crop hay. All had been safely tucked away in the now-flaming barn.

A frantic neighbor came rushing up to Henry and told him to start the diesel tractor standing nearby, so they could unload a flaming self-unloading wagon. It took Henry a few minutes to figure out the controls and then off they went. Other neighbors joined them to help move the cattle to an empty barn near Rush Lake, and then feed and milk them.

My mother-in-law and I went home to milk our own cows, all the while thinking about the calamity that had befallen our good neighbors.

That was over 17 years ago. What happened to Arnie and

Opal (his wife), and Dick? Does a fire permanently damage a farmer?

The Berlin Journal account of that fateful day quotes Arnie as saying, "Yes, we're going to build up again, land is no good without a barn. Life is more than money for me."

Opal recalls being "so scared" as she was baby-sitting Dick's daughters, ages 3 and 5, in the house. They wanted to go outside. She stood in the door way, wondering if the house was even safe, and worried about how Arnie would be able to handle this.

Arnie and Dick were baling on neighbor Elmer Cluppert's farm. When Opal saw Arnie walking across the yard, and heard him giving orders, then she knew he was all right. He was in control.

"For the life of me, I still don't know how Dick moved that spreader," Opal reminisces. "It had a long tongue, and he pulled it uphill—by hand—in order to get the calves and bull out."

Shortly after Thanksgiving the new barn was up, and with much neighborhood help, the yard was cleaned up. But it wasn't easy, and it wasn't cheap. Like so many farmers, even today, the Nummerdors failed to update their insurance. The old barn was covered at one-third of the replacement cost.

"But we had it paid back in four years," Opal says proudly. "We had a few good years in there."

She didn't say, but I know those years included a lot of hard work.

"As disastrous as the fire was, it turned out to be better for Arnie's health," Opal remembers, "because the new barn didn't have so much dust and mold." Arnie took shots daily for allergies.

After the farm got back on its feet, Dick, his wife, and daughters left for another occupation. In four years Arnie and Opal sold the farm, "Because we had a good buyer."

"Besides," Opal adds, "I couldn't take the hard work much longer. I was becoming very arthritic."

But Arnie stayed close to the land he loved. This was to the benefit of the farmers for whom he not only did field work, but also with whom he shared his laugh, his sense of humor, and his calm and logical outlook on life.

A fire may have set them back for a while, but it couldn't smother the strong spirit of these farmers. Looking back, Opal sums it up by saying, "You never realize how good people are until tragedy strikes."

January, 1991

View From The Haymow

Just under the gable peak of our barn is a small rectangular window. Framed in white and set on one corner, with an arrowed weather vane rising from the roof above, it gives the barn its own quaint character.

In passing one day, movement at that window caught my eye. It was a black and white kitten jumping at the screened opening in pursuit of a moth. The mow was full of straw just up to the window, and so formed a nice window seat for her. It was a kitten I did not recognize. Must be Miney's.

I saw the large area of matted hair around her nipples and heard her demanding cries for food, and so I knew the rail-thin Miney was still nursing large size kittens. Fear of the dog kept her from bringing them down. Usually when barn cats realize they can no longer nurse their young, they bring them to the cat dish. Last winter one of Miney's half-grown kittens froze to death up in the mow.

Weeks went by and the kittens did not join the feline assembly that gathers at the cat dish, waiting for waste milk after each milking. I decided it was up to me to see if there was even a way for mother to get them out.

The route to ascend appeared safe. Wooden rungs built into the wall up to mow level and bracing 4 X 4's running at angles to main beams provided a good grasp, and then a place for my foot while I pulled myself up onto the top beam. I paused to catch my breath and wistfully recollected how nimbly I used to scamper up here. Looking down at the barn floor way below—it seemed so far. Would it be as easy to lower my weight as it was to pull it up? Would my foot find the toe-hold in the perpendicular climb?

Once Upon A Farm

First to the kittens. I climbed the bales that pyramided into the peak of the barn and crawled over to the window. Not a kitten in sight. Only a young sparrow flailing itself against the screen, searching for freedom. Stupid bird. All she had to do was fly across the mow to the open big doors, but she could see only her way.

Sitting on the bale window seat, I gazed at the scene below. It looked so different from up here. Red geraniums in the green grass of the yard glowed vibrant in the morning sun. Nearby, the dog slept peacefully with his black nose across one paw, waiting for the day's action to begin. Birds sailed across the lawn and on the hillside the corn stood tall and green. All was quiet—serene—far removed from me. If I didn't make the descent I might never be part of that scene again.

While in the haymow checking on kittens, Lois fears she might never again be part of this scene.

The picture of a young farm wife flashed before my eyes. She had come on crutches and showed me the long scar on a swollen ankle that crushed beneath her when she fell from her barn mow. (I could hear Henry cursing the cats and my stupidity.)

Oh well, where were those cats? I crawled over to the next mow, not quite so full. Miney stared at me from the edge. I became motionless. Miney "talked" to her kittens. Soon an angora duplicate of the mother frisked to her side. I saw another tail bobbing behind the next layer of bales which formed descending ledges into the slant of the roof. There was ample room to nurse and play. I edged closer, Miney jumped down to a beam and then a lower one which ran across to the adjoining granary. An easy route to carry kittens if she ever put her mind to it. The kittens dissolved into the hay. Not a clue as to where, but I knew that at Miney's call they would reappear and she would care for them. I was satisfied. There was nothing more I could do.

From this point I could see across the open mow floor and through the open chute above the cows. Far below they were resting comfortably, re-chewing their breakfast fiber. Would I touch those cows again? I became apprehensive about my descent. "Lord, I'm sorry about the harsh words and gossip I shared yesterday. Give me another chance." Would I lie in a hospital bed for weeks and not see the greens of the hillside? The world looked so beautiful from up here. Why did there have to be greed, and hate, and strife?

Well, here goes. I stood on the beam dividing the mows. It was wide and solid beneath my foot, with bales towering straight up on my right, on my left the open chute, far below the concrete floor. Realizing the clumsiness the years have presented me, I quickly dropped to my knees and anchored my hands in the bales. My toe searched for the angle of wood. There it was.

Slowly, making sure each grasp was secure; I came back safely to earth, feeling like a new person, fantasizing about bringing the leaders of world governments to our haymow—for the view.

September, 1990

It's Easier To Grow Corn Than Flowers!

To a farm man's eye—corn is beautiful. There is something about growing corn. A nice stand gives a man a deep satisfied feeling. It's a beauty to him that can't compare to much other plant life.

But for me, the real challenge is growing flower beds on the farm. The battle starts in spring when I first find the courage to set out plants or lay expensive hybrid seeds in the warming earth. No sooner than I set marigolds in the planter, some critter snips them off, leaving only naked stems.

I can't put seeds under the yard light, because the cats love that loose soil for their "daily duty." So I try to keep geraniums over winter and set them out, but often the cat's play or the dog's chase break the anemic stems before they have a chance to re-adjust to outdoor living.

Giving in to the animals, I plant only shrubs and "Snow-on-the-Mountain" all around the house. Even this they dig under for cool damp shade when temperatures soar.

A bed of red and white petunias framed the barn nicely—until the heifers got out! Their big hooves made monster footprints in the soft ground and dragged and broke the tender plants.

The Highbush Cranberry was doing very well for its first summer last year in my bird-attracting-garden, until my husband plowed the adjacent vegetable garden.

"Why do you think that broom handle was stuck next to it?" I asked in disbelief as I trimmed the broken branches.

"Didn't see it."

This summer I had one pride and joy, one of those expensive New Guinea Impatiens. It came into its full glory about the same time hubby decided to have the septic system pumped out. The cherry-red blooms surrounded by lamium cascaded from a black butcher's kettle, which was cemented to the cover of the septic tank. All safe and sound where nothing could get at it.

I watched from the kitchen window as hubby very neatly attached chains to the side handles of the kettle, and using the skid-loader lifted the whole works with the chain hooked over the bucket. Not a leaf quivered as he gently set the kettle on the lawn. I admired my husband's cleverness, as I heard him yell to the pumper man, "I'll go get the other tank open. I know you're in a hurry."

Ten minutes later I looked out the window again. I couldn't believe it! The skid-loader had lost hydraulic pressure and the big bucket had dropped, settling itself squarely across the top of the flower kettle. Only the trailing lamium vines were sticking straight out from underneath the bucket as if in screaming protest. I was just sick. Rushing outside I tried to lift the bucket, but couldn't find the right pedal. To my dismay, I managed to slide the bucket back and forth a few times before finally lifting it off the mashed mess.

Henry came back, "I forgot about it settling," he said sheepishly. Then he reminded me of a previous instance when I was at fault for forgetting. "Remember the rototiller tines?"

He was referring to the time I asked him to cut the weeds in the garden with his green chopper. I had forgotten the rototiller tines were still lying in the row where I had removed them. They tore the guts out of his $6000 machine.

"Maybe gardening and farming are not compatible after all," I said in resignation, leaning against the maple tree. Looking up at the crimsons, golds, and russets of the leaves, I decided to relax and enjoy Mother Nature's handiwork. I could hardly compete.

On the hill behind us the long leafy arms of corn stalks waved at me tauntingly.

October, 1987

Jerry Gives Me Sight

"You're just on the farm? You don't work?"

I cringed at the question asked by an old classmate. It's like one step below "just a housewife." Two of the most important jobs in the world, housewife and farmer, have somehow gotten to the bottom of the list.

A recent visitor opened my eyes. When I was in my early

Once Upon A Farm

teens, my mother took in a nephew for several years. The victim of a divorce, he needed a stable situation, and our small midwest farm was his refuge. Jerry was two years younger than I. My mother sent him with me on all dates with Henry. This action proved very effective. Eventually Jerry's mother remarried and settled in California. He went to join her—much to Henry's delight.

We hadn't seen him for years until last weekend. He phoned from Chicago where he was attending a fancy wedding. I didn't have time to fuss or do anything special. Just chores and meals as usual.

Jerry went with me to the barn. He marveled at the size of a three-day-old calf, and how different our milking procedure was from my pa's. His memories were of an open pail and an open strainer. "You mean the milk is always inside stainless steel from the cow to the bulk tank?"

For supper we had chicken dumpling soup (the kind my mother used to make). "That smells like chicken soup," he said in disbelief as he settled his huge frame at our kitchen table. At dinner next day he was amazed that the delicious cut of meat was just a pot roast from one of our steers.

Jerry stood for a long time studying the collage of farm photos on our family room wall. It includes such things as the girls on the roof of the corn crib the day they helped Dad build it; Dad and son goofing off at the swimming pond; picking stones together; showing 4-H calves; and having fun with cats and dogs.

Jerry wandered around outside. He took photos of the blue jays at the feeder, the cows eating at the bunk in the barnyard, the milk truck coming down the drive, and the wire cribs chocked full of golden corn. (He wanted pictures of snow.)

"Are those geese I hear?"he said, his pale face breaking into contours of joy. "That's a sound I haven't heard for a long time."

On Sunday Jerry packed his suitcase saying wistfully, "This has been the highlight of my trip. I wish I had a few more days. Now I go back to the California smog. Every day it's a long city drive to a meaningless job."

Seeing things from his point of view made me appreciate

what I had. That afternoon I took a little more pride in feeding my calves. After all, they were to grow up to be foster mothers of the human race. I thought about my lowly job and realized housewives and farmers not only create life, but more importantly, support, nurture, and control the quality of that life. I wasn't trying to glorify a situation I couldn't change. I was just realizing its true value.

It's easy to feel defeated when headlines scream about the burden of bountiful harvests and tremendous carryovers. They are not burdens. They are this country's insurance policy.

Huge food supplies are allowed to insure low food prices and full stomachs for all. When people go to bed hungry it's usually due to poverty, not lack of food.

As rural Americans we should be proud of our abundant food supply and of the efficient way in which we produce it. We should prefer a full bin to an empty one, and prefer all the milk we can consume to rationing. The farm programs (and there will always be some in one form or another) are a way of sharing the burden of plenty.

I waved good-bye to Jerry and felt very content. Not only content—I was proud! Yes, I work. I work on our farm.

November, 1987

Bloom Where You Are Planted And Enjoy The Season

It was already late summer when I saw the little sprig of marigold leaf in the crack between the cement sidewalk and the garage foundation. I yanked out some of the creeping weeds nearby and let it be, completely forgetting about it.

On the other side of the house in rich soil and southern sunlight, I spent all spring and summer pampering a new type of perennial geranium plant. I watered it daily and worked peat moss around its roots to keep it moist. Then I protected it with a circle of rocks. It died.

Meanwhile in the hot, dry concrete of the garage area, frequented daily by the dog, kids, wayward basketballs, and car exhaust, the little overlooked plant thrived. It was not until it burst into a blaze of orange that I finally noticed it. The man of the house even noticed it! I took its picture!

So much like people. Some are pampered and nourished, given every opportunity, and yet for all good purposes—they are dead; having brought little joy to those that pass by in their lives and making minimal contributions to society.

At the same time some common folks go about their daily lives struggling against odds, performing menial tasks, seemingly unnoticed. Sometimes planted in undesirable locations, they persist and bloom anyhow, bringing cheer to those around them and brightening their corner of the world.

Some may feel inferior, like onions in a petunia patch, but their true colors shine through. Because of their reliability and perseverance, their contributions are finally noticed and bouquets are made. Sometimes it is not until their bloom is gone that we realize how much they contributed.

I hated to see the frost come and take away the bright red salvias and zinnias of summer. It meant a season was over—much like the first time a son beats his father in a race—a season is passing. I was not ready for signs of fall. My heart sank when the first golden leaves fell, as when my first hair turned grey. But the season is here—so enjoy it.

This season has some good points. The golds, rusts, and auburn colors of changing leaves and crops are warm and glowing. There is something satisfying in harvesting golden ears of corn, orange squash, and red apples. We lay up a larder of supplies for man and beast—reveling in the fruits of our labors, insulating against the future.

In life, we may not yet be ready to slow down or to "change seasons," but it happens. There is good in it. A warm and contented feeling comes from the accomplishment of projects completed, surrounded by a grown family. There is hope that some insulation has been made for the future.

With the accumulation of years, like a glowing harvest, comes the gathering of wisdom and patience and foresight. It is the season to share those fruits, spreading them to those in "other seasons" who may be having a little trouble getting their "blossoms" to open.

It was late in the season when the plucky little marigold was seeded, by mistake, and in the wrong place.

It bloomed anyhow.

October, 1991

That Time Of Year

Henry is nervous. It's that time of year. There is only so much time before the workable ground becomes frozen like rock, and plowing days are ended. There are only so many days before frigid temperatures dictate an end to outside repair work. Cows, machinery, and buildings have to be fortified for winter.

Year-end accounting, tax work, and just the "thought of winter" loom like dark monsters blocking our view. That view became a little clearer recently as I gazed out the kitchen window at the blue jays stashing sunflower seeds from my feeder. The blackbird with only one leg teetered on the edge of the platform, courageously seeking nourishment.

My gaze wandered to the cardboard "thankoffering" coin box on the window sill, brightly painted with reasons to give thanks at this time of year. Studying the words, I realized none of the things listed could be bought.

I thought about each item:

HEALTH—to be healthy enough to work and to have honest work to do. I don't appreciate it enough.

LOVE—to have your family or friend express it once in a while in one way or another . . . is wonderful.

PEACE—it seems threatened at times, but it's still here.

CHARITY—whether giving it or receiving it . . . a reason to be thankful.

LIFE—itself a blessing.

HOPE—for a farmer it returns each season, and keeps us jumping hurdles and in the race.

FAITH—the gift that gives meaning to life.

JOY—to be able to find it in simple things like a clean closet, a husband's hug, or a newborn calf, is pure bounty.

Once Upon A Farm

Thanking God for a better view, I slipped a coin into the box. It's that time of year . . . to take inventory, and to say along with the psalmist, "I thank thee, Lord."

November, 1988

Two Men

Keith's hair was smartly styled, fluffed and full it lay in perfect layers, setting off the pinkish-white skin of his face. Wire-rimmed glasses and a firm square jaw gave him the look of the businessman he was.

Across the table at the agribusiness dinner meeting, an unruly wisp of Carl's hair swung across his forehead. The wind and sun had styled it, as well as his skin which in color and texture resembled leather.

Keith's long slim fingers nervously fidgeted with his company pen. His ring finger was adorned with a diamond-set band, and the squared nails were nicely manicured.

Veins stood out on Carl's thick brown hands. Over-sized knuckles and crooked fingers ended in wide, broken nails. One thumb nail was black and loosening from injury. His plain wedding band lay in the dresser-drawer at home. His occupation was too dangerous to wear it daily. After rushing through morning milking, and chores that included treating a down cow and a broken hose on the tractor, the last thing Carl thought of was putting on a wedding ring for appearance in public.

Keith looked smart in a suit of dark grey with white shirt and red tie.

The plain grey knot of Carl's tie did not snuggle up tight against a neck that rebelled against it, but hung loose on a blue sport shirt.

Keith's young eyes were bright with interest and observation of the various speakers.

Carl's eyes crinkled at the corners when they joked over dinner, but now they were half-closed. They had been open since 4:00 a.m., and above a full stomach were slowly losing the struggle to focus on the speaker or the message, both of which he had heard before.

Two men—so different in many ways, both needed by agriculture.

Carl was a producer. He worked with animals, and land and machines. He loved the outdoors and being able to make some of his own decisions. Because his occupation gave him opportunity to have his family work with him, and because he felt he was doing something worthwhile and taking good care of the land, he felt committed to it—in spite of the poor dollar return.

Keith produced profit. He worked with numbers and programs, getting more sales and fighting the competition. He was learning a lot about people as well as his product. The company pushed him to sell more—no matter what. They had a whole bag full of tricks for him to implement.

Agriculture needs producers, but it needs product research, industry development, and sales and marketing of products as well.

Carl is becoming more like Keith every day. His clumsy fingers have conquered the computer keys. He is spending more time on numbers, programs, and cash flow.

Keith is becoming more like Carl in that more and more businessmen are owning farmland. However, the non-operator knows little of the realities or conscience of farming the land.

Consider that at the end of 1988 only 4% of U.S. farm land owners held 47% of the land. Of the total owners (2.9 million) 44% were non-operators who held 41% of the land.

As the number of farm land owners shrinks, decisions about land use, conservation, inputs and resource quality are made by an even smaller minority of the overall population.

We are in grave danger. The shrinking number of farms and land owners will contribute further to the decline of rural communities. It will affect how food is produced and sold, at what cost, and to whom.

We need both Keith and Carl. We need them both to perform their jobs well and in consideration of their fellowman. But we need to keep the "Carls" on the land.

January, 1992

P. WOUTS-Hanson

About Critters

The Worth Of A Sparrow

"If it weren't for the birds and our aches and pains, what would we talk about?" an elderly man said to his friend as they visited in the grocery store.

That's the truth for a lot of people, especially this time of year. Thank God for the birds. Nothing brightens a dull morning more than the flash of a red cardinal or the sassiness of a blue jay. A bold chickadee flits at the feeder, sharply dressed in black and white headgear. He stays when you approach and you know you have a friend.

There are at least 20 million bird watchers in the United States. The sale of bird seed mixtures has now become a multimillion-dollar business; as the sport of bird watching attracts people of all ages from all walks of life—and I'm one of them.

Not that there are any starving birds on the farm. The blue jays that come to "pig out" within five minutes after I put out sunflower seeds, pry themselves away from the corn cribs to do it. There's usually some grist spilled by the feed bin, and always "slightly processed" grains in the manure pile or in the "pies" dotting the heifer yard. Not to mention an abundance of weed seeds scattered throughout the fields.

But to attract them to my window view, I put out seeds and suet. Along with all the other "birders," I am fascinated by the visual treat they offer, along with the reaffirmation of the joy and goodness of living.

The upside-down antics of the nuthatch awakens my daydreaming, as he shares the suet with the hairy and downy woodpeckers. A red-bellied woodpecker perches on the edge of the platform feeder. Just as I'm thinking he has more red on his head than on his belly, he teeters backwards a bit as if to show me the rosy glow on his tummy that gives him his name.

Once Upon A Farm

I haven't seen many "snowbirds" this year. I guess the weather has been too nice for them. But a few pairs of tree sparrows have decided they would rather spend the winter in our yard than in Canada. I watch them play a game of tag in and out of the base of the huge old lilac bush. In a wink one is on the feeder, feverishly scratching the remaining millet. Marked by his jaunty rusty cap and black spot at center breast, he gobbles up seeds looking this way and that. Flitting his tail, he is a bundle of nervous energy.

A few goldfinch in their drab winter color enjoy the sunflower seeds as much as the thistle seed mix. Each day I study them carefully. When the greenish-grey starts to take on a tinge of yellow, I know spring is not far off.

A flock of sparrows flutters to the ground underneath the feeder. I look at them with scorn, and then check myself. Just because there are so many of them, does that make any of them want to live less? Because they are not beautiful or have special singing talents, is that why they are not important to me?

Yet, like good friends, they are always there, no matter what the weather or the season. Always busy, going about their business of raising families, happily chirping in the only song they know.

How much like God's common people of the world, I thought. There are a lot of them too, often looked down on and scorned. That doesn't mean they lack pride, or love their families less, or want any less for them. Yet they find joy and meaning in their lives.

A Bible verse came to mind, "Are not two sparrows sold for a penny? And not one of them will fall to the ground without your Father's will." (Matthew 10:29)

March, 1989

Motherhood

"Meenie" the Ma cat comes to eat at the old frying pan that serves as a cat dish in the barn alley. She keeps a close watch for the animal that terrifies her, our huge dog, Bear.

Meenie is the lone survivor of a trio of kittens born eight years ago, Eenie, Meenie, and Moe. Yesterday her belly looked as if she swallowed a balloon. Today she is skinny. Her usually smooth coat is matted and in disarray. She knows it is milking time and has risked leaving her newborn babes a few minutes to nourish herself.

There is concern and anxiety in the way she eats quickly, stopping often and looking back over her shoulder. I scratch her ears, gently lifting her front legs. Four pink nipples protrude from white fur that has been pressed down by tiny paws. There must be four kittens. Each has its own "bottle."

The black Bear appears around the corner and Meenie scales the pen wall, perching on a cross beam. Experience has taught her this is a safe place. Bear swings his plume of a tail and whines in anticipation. He remembers the fun chases she has given him and wishes she would come down and "go for it." He would never hurt her, but she doesn't know that.

Cats are very patient animals. Meenie will wait until Bear runs off to other pursuits. Then she will sneak back to that special place where she has hidden her newborn. It could be between old bales in the back part of the hay mow, or a nest burrowed into the chopped corn stalks remaining on a wagon in the shed. It will be a place where she finds protection and privacy. I have tried trailing cats to find their young. They always outsmart me, sitting down in the middle of the shed, calmly licking their paws, and giving me the smirkish look that only cats can give.

We may not see Meenie's kittens until they are half-grown and her milk runs dry. She will take them on field trips, coaxing them to follow and stalk and wait. They will be good mousers, learning from their mother.

Watching her, I remembered back to last June when she brought me one of her litter. She carried it an unusual way, her mouth anchored in the fur *underneath* the neck. Usually mother cats carry their young by the back of the neck, with the kitten's feet dangling helplessly. This way they can't kick or struggle while Mother carries them to what she considers a safer place.

The kitten she was bringing me was almost too big to be

carried. She half dragged it across the walkway in the calf barn and laid it at my feet, crying piteously. It was the mottled gray one of a litter that also included two solid black and two black and whites. It was the one that spit so hard at me when I found them in the hay mow. Fearing a live burial by the new hay crop, I had moved them to a corner of the granary.

The kitten at my feet did not move. Mother touched her nose to its head, its sides, and then its tail, moving over the entire limp body. The kitten lay still. The mother called in her special low pitched "Merrow" that even I recognized as her call to her young, meaning "come to me."

The kitten did not respond. I bent down and picked up the cold little body. What had happened? I don't know. A Tom cat? Disease? There were no clues. I took the dead kitten away from its mourning mother.

For hours she ran back and forth through the barn— searching and calling. She jumped out the window and in a few minutes was back in. She went into the silo room. Ignoring Bear and her fear of him, she walked to the middle of the platform and again called, "Come to me." She went out the door and came back in.

Finally, evening came. Meenie took a little milk at the dish. Then she climbed the beams that led to the granary. It was time for the mother to turn her attention to the living kittens that needed her.

May, 1990

Birthing On Grass:
More Picturesque Than Practical

Our marsh is a maze of humps and water filled bogs. You try to step from hump to hump but often a foot slips off to the sucking black ooze below. While swatting mosquitoes and deer flies it's difficult to pick out the soggy trail cleared by the heifers.

Somehow I hopscotched through it, searching for the cow that didn't come up to the yard. A glance to my right and I saw her, dozing on a grassy area that was higher and drier. With the newborn calf snuggled next to her side, they looked like a picture right off the farm calendar. Except that the artist forgot to put in the mosquitoes and the mud. He also forgot to depict how cow and calf travel to the barn.

Walk? Simple enough. The calf can walk within an hour or two of birth. So just chase the cow, and calf will follow. Not that simple. No way is Mom going to move more than two feet from her calf. No matter how I holler and slap, she only does a pivot step and circles back to the baby.

The baby sees no reason to leave Mother's side. (After all that's where she got her first free lunch.) She's not going to be pushed or led into any unknown spaces, and effectively applies the brakes with braced feet. We are getting nowhere fast.

After 10 minutes of my prodding and screaming, we are only going in circles and not much closer to the barnyard. This will never do, so I direct my arm swinging and vocal efforts to the direction of the farm yard.

Eventually two men mount the humps and grudgingly come to my rescue. Henry and Dennis look about as happy as when the manure spreader breaks with a full load on it. It's not easy to carry a calf through the marsh. We all blame each other.

"What'd ya let her calve out here for?"

"She wasn't due yet."

"Wasn't even bagged out."

Promises are made to watch prospective mothers more closely. The baby heifer is properly named, "Marsha."

Lois bottle feeds twins born in the marsh.

Once Upon A Farm

In spite of our vows, two weeks later another birth catches us unaware. This time the mother is in the barnyard feedlot area (mosquitoes, but no bogs). When Oralu didn't come in with the other cows, I knew something was up and found her standing under the old oak tree in the farthest corner of the lot. Dangling membranes announced that a birth had occurred, but where was the calf?

A quick glance around the feedlot revealed only cow pies and a few tough weeds. Oralu stayed in one area, close to the fence. There the matted grass, wet with fluids, indicated this had been her birthing bed.

Sure enough, the little one must have gotten to his feet on the wrong side of the fence! I walked through the tall grass there. Nothing. Enlisting a search party, the four of us walked through the strips of corn and oats that contour the hillside nearby. We walked through the patch of scrubby trees behind the feed lot and along the ditch that divided field and marsh. It soon became too dark to see anymore. No baby was to be found.

My sleep that night was interrupted by visions of a dead calf lying in water at the ditch bottom, or scenes of wobbly legs stumbling through tall grass onto the highway.

In the morning I stood looking out over the hill, wondering which way to go. There was nothing moving, only a few blackbirds winging their way with rasping cries. One perched on a stem of oats. I again searched the area next to the fence and then gazed up the hill.

The blackbird was still there—motionless. That was strange. Was it sick? I set out in that direction and was within 20 feet of it before I realized it was not a blackbird at all. It was the ear of a calf!

There he was, curled up like a cat in front of a fireplace. The big bull calf was sound asleep, his head tucked around with one ear sticking up above the oats.

The lost was found! We must have walked right past him. With joy, the men hauled this one home in the truck.

The next cow to calve is going into the maternity pen two weeks early! It won't make as pretty a picture, but it's a lot easier on the midwives.

July, 1990

In Stitches—But Not Laughing

The calf was a beauty, strong and tall with good set to her legs. We were really happy to have our first heifer out of Denise. Especially since she was listed as one of the top 10,000 type production cows in the country.

I took special care to dip her navel in iodine and feed a nipple bottle of colostrum as soon as she was born. "Tornado" is the name I gave her after her sire, Southwind, and my whirlwind expectations of her.

When she ran a little temp and started coughing and scouring, we hit her with antibiotics. There was a little swelling under her belly and the medicine reduced this, but the navel remained an unsightly lump. The vet said it wasn't much of a rupture. He suggested maybe we could avoid surgery by pushing it up every day and irritating the area, so that more blood would come to the area and heal it. No such luck.

Surgery was scheduled. "There's always the chance that an animal might not come out of heavy sedation," said Dr. Bill. "That's why we wanted to avoid surgery on this valuable animal. We won't give her any more than we have to."

The operating table consisted of six bales piled three deep, side by side; the main purpose being to bring the animal up to easy working height.

Dennis had already clipped the area. The vet slipped a needle of anesthetic into a neck vein. Tornado was soon as floppy as a rag doll.

Just so no reflex movements would misdirect the surgeon's scalpel, we took our positions; Dennis on the hind legs, Henry held the front legs, and I held her head to keep it from dangling over the edge of the bales as she lay on her back.

More injections, this time all around the navel area to prevent any feeling of pain for Tornado. Then Dr. Bill proceeded to follow some sanitizing procedures. He soaped and scrubbed the calf's belly until it was cleaner than a newborn babe's. He laid clean cloths over her chest and rear legs. On himself he put surgical gloves and then disinfected his bare arms.

Just like Mayo Clinic, I thought to myself. Even if this is a plain old calf barn. Shivers crept through my body, partly due to my nervous state and partly because it was below freezing out here. Keeping our calves in the cold keeps them healthier. Rather than stress the calf by changing its environment, we stressed the vet instead.

He quickly snipped away the dangling skin that covered the rupture. "I don't know what we have here. It's not a normal rupture."

My body trembled a little more.

"Is it serious?" Henry asked, suddenly becoming very sober, after ten minutes of the usual banter.

"She's the only heifer calf Denise ever had," I said.

"Let's just say we're in unknown waters for now," Dr. Bill said. His fingers kept probing the hole in the calf's belly and pulling on the thick muscle-like thumb sticking into the air. "It must be part of the umbilical cord that became infected and wouldn't let the opening close. Part of the intestine is adhered to it. What a mess!"

"You're making me nervous," Henry said.

"You just have to take it in stride, like everything else," Dr. Bill said. His fingers kept on working, probing, sorting, and snipping. Finally the mass was sorted and cut loose. He tossed it on a bale. "Now if I were in a modern medical center, I could send that down to pathology and have it analyzed before proceeding any farther. I'll look at it later. I bet it's filled with pus. You must have had this animal on antibiotics for a period, which cauterized the infection."

Time to start the repair. A syringe full of penicillin went into the opening.

"Is she going to be okay?"

"Seems like it."

I stopped shivering.

Stainless steel sutures went on the inside, were pulled tight, and tied securely. "I don't plan on those ever coming undone. They stay with her," said the Doc. Cat gut knots went on the next layer. "The white corpuscles will carry those away in a month or two."

The outside flab of skin was anchored in the middle with a solid knot and the gap closed with stitches to each end of the opening, about 25 in all. Those would be snipped in about two weeks when the incision was healed.

Using it like a magic wand, Dr. Bill waved a can of aerosol spray over the wound, bathing it in healing yellow coating. "There you are folks! She needs to be alone for at least a week."

Tornado was carefully carried to a clean bed of straw. We propped her legs under her. Her nose sank into the straw. Her eyes were open, but not seeing. In a few hours she staggered to her feet. The next morning she was bright and alert. She continues to be a beauty.

Mayo Clinic doesn't have anything on the country vet!

February, 1991

Parton's Present

It was my birthday, but we weren't celebrating until evening, so Dennis and I decided to move heifers.

When the calves become too big for the pens in our old horse barn, they are loaded onto a horse trailer (left over from our daughter's "horse" days) and moved to the old cow barn across the road. It's wide open so they go in and out as they please, getting both sunshine and yet protection.

For my "babies" it is their first time outside. Until now, at about eight months of age, all they have seen is a pen with strong boards, a feed manger, a drinking cup, and a few creatures like themselves and me. So it takes some prodding and guiding with gates and broom handle to convince them to enter the unknown.

Today one was particularly dumb. In naming Dolly's daughter "Parton" I was anticipating a lot of milk! But she was dumb—one of those with closed eyes, and ears, and mind, oblivious to waving hands and thumps on the noggin with my broom. Dennis finally put a gate along side her across the barn sill and practically lifted her bodily into the trailer.

When we got the trailer over to the other barn, she wouldn't get out! We did some hollering and pushing before she backed out of the trailer door. All of a sudden she found herself in this *big* yard, with bright sunshine, and a fence of wire instead of wide boards.

Dolly Parton took off—like the star of a Spanish bull fight, with full speed she charged the fence. There was an electric wire, but by the time she felt it she was already tangled in the net wire behind it. In a minute Parton had the whole world for her yard. She ambled across the lawn, looking this way and that, then decided to check out Brewer's hayfield to the south. There was a fence there too but that didn't stop her—just plunge right in and climb and kick until you are free. The cross road lay to the east, and a corn field to the south straight ahead. Parton chose to go west. Thank heavens. At least I could dismiss the visions I had of chasing her down Highway 116. (No one else was home to help.)

By now her face was slashed and I wondered how many teats were still in place. She trotted slowly next to the cornfield. I took off in a trot also, trying to get ahead of her. She was a little chubby too, but in better shape than I was. I slowed to a walk, calling to her. She came across the hayfield towards me, with Dennis in pursuit. She let us get next to her. But how do we convince her to go back to the buildings now 400 yards away?

Dennis took off his belt and slipped it around her neck. At least he had a handle on her, but she had never been led before—and wasn't about to start now. Now what? Pull and shove and make her jump the fence again? I didn't like the thought of that. "Dennis," I said, "this heifer has the highest index of any that we have, at +955. Losing a teat won't do much for that."

"She's going to high index herself right to heaven,"he said, his patience fast disappearing.

I found a section of the old fence that was broken where the deer had been crossing. Only the bottom wire was strung, but it was over a steep decline, and Parton firmly planted her feet, clearly stating, "No, thank you."

"Tell you what," Dennis brainstormed. "Can you go get the trailer and we'll load her up again out here?"

"You remember how hard it was to get her on the first

time?"I said. "Besides, can I even drive that tractor?" "It's still running. The brakes are set, on the right. Put the left gear in two, and the right gear in three."

I took the long hike back, leaving Dennis and Parton to argue. By the time I got my boots off (no wonder I couldn't run) and closed a gate, I forgot what he said about gears. There was only a I and a II on the left. Being in a hurry I chose II. The gears on the right weren't marked, so I just found a likely slot. Slowly releasing the clutch I moved forward at good speed, proud of myself. Memories of long hours spent baling and chopping came back to me. Tractors and I are not total strangers.

Dennis and Parton were still in the middle of the field. She didn't even panic when the tractor got close, thereby redeeming herself and proving she wasn't wild, just a bit disoriented.

A rope halter inside proved helpful in winching her back into the trailer. That halter stayed on her for the next 24 hours. We sprayed her wounds with yellow Furox. Dennis said, "Now she looks like a yellow zombie."

A dew claw was skinned, her chest cut, and face zigzagged, but Dolly Parton's yet undeveloped udder was intact. She would be just fine.

While I was dining with my family that evening, Parton was tied to the water fountain, being given ample time to survey her new surroundings.

Her escapades were one birthday present I won't forget.

September, 1991

Never On Sunday

"All right girls, behave yourselves—you know me," I said, walking slowly through the heifer lot. I was looking for Purity, a mostly white heifer that had been in heat the evening before.

All heads were up and eyes on me. This lot of "teenagers" wasn't used to having people on foot amongst them. Tractors pulling feed wagons—yes. They even bellered whenever they heard a tractor nearby, thinking their feed was coming. But people on foot meant fun and games.

The ones that had been taking a nap in the early morning coolness were soon on their feet. Party, my special pet as a calf, was soon right behind me trying to chew on my shirt tails. A few livelier ones put their heads down towards me and danced their back ends around in half circles, as if to say, "Let's play—you run and we'll chase you."

I was not to oblige. I kept my slow, measured pace. Of course, Purity had to be at the farthest end of the lot, her head tucked alongside her body, sound asleep on a pad of dried grass. She was all tuckered out from her nocturnal activities.

A few cocky ones ran past her and she quickly came to life. With the help of Dennis, I started walking her towards the barn, trying to keep her close to the fence so she couldn't circle back. The farther we got, the more nervous she became. Three of her friends followed her into the barnyard. We hooked the chain on a temporary gate locking the others out.

Henry joined in our efforts and we edged her to the open barn door. She zipped right past. When we brought them back again her three friends went in, but not Purity. (Whoever named her that?) On her next trip across the barnyard she found herself alone and really panicked. Picking up steam like a bull she charged the gate, pulling out the temporary steel post.

"That's it!" Henry said. "Get the tractor, Dennis. We've got to make a barricade."

It took them ten minutes to erect a wall of tractors and gates pieced and parked together. As if she knew she didn't have a chance of escape, she walked right in—right in the barn that is. To get her in a stanchion would be another matter.

First she put her head on the right of the stanchion, and then on the left. Then she stuck it underneath the belly of the cow next to her.

"We've got to get her bred," Henry said, "or she'll be old enough to vote before she has her first calf."

"Just give her time," Dennis suggested. I could tell by the

way his huge hands were fidgeting at his sides though, that he'd just as soon pick her up and throw her in the stanchion.

"C'mon, Baby," I cooed, dumping a scoop-full of grain in front of the stanchion opening. She sniffed and reached what she could with a long lick of an extended tongue. The taste got the best of her. Her head was in. Using the cow next to her as a screen, Henry reached the latch over her head with a scraper handle and she was locked.

When this knowledge registered on her minuscule brain, she protested. First by pulling back and bracing her front feet. This gave her a headache where the stanchion pinched her ears. So then she tried getting on her knees, almost standing on her head.

"I don't remember her being this wild as a calf," I said. As if she heard me or finally gave up, she quieted down for the procedure of breeding. Even the magnet shoved down her throat and the vaccine shots didn't rile her too much.

I opened the door for her to join her friends again. "See you in nine months, Purity, when you have that calf. Don't come in heat again."

She bolted through the door and kicked both hind feet sideways at me as if to have the last word.

The heifer had taken up 45 extra minutes of a Sunday morning chore routine, which is usually shortened as much as possible. We walked into church five minutes late, breakfast-less, and showered-but-still-sweating.

People probably thought we overslept.

June, 1988

A Handicap Turned Blessing

"I'll never have a cat in the house." Those were my exact words—about thirteen years ago.

"Mom, Kathy's cat had a pure white baby kitten. Her mom won't let her keep it. Can I bring it home? Please?" Our daughter, Val, had asked way back then.

My reply was firm. "No, we already have too many cats in the barn, messin' in the grain and under my feet all the time."

Once Upon A Farm

Then a few days later the old Springer dog lay on the kittens of Val's favorite barn cat and smothered them. Tears running down her cheeks, she begged again for the white kitten. This time I couldn't say no. "But," I added, "she has to stay in the barn."

And so she did. However, it seemed she had no fear. The little white kitten wouldn't get out of the way when the cows walked in behind her. The lime cart rattling down the platform didn't frighten her to move. We hollered at her to get out of the way, but she ignored us. Finally, we realized the truth. She wasn't brave. She was deaf.

"Mom, she'll be killed out there," Val pleaded again. "Can she come in the house?"

My vow was broken and "Lady Josephine" (as Kathy had named her) became our house cat. She was never much to look at. Besides having a scrawny face and short hair, she had one green eye and one blue eye and always fell over on her back when she scratched her ear. The same genes that gave her white hair and the blue eye (therefore deafness), also presented her with balance problems.

Val spent a lot of time with "Jo-Jo," but as with many kid's pets, she became Mom's responsibility. So for over 12 years I've been scooping out the litter box and vacuuming cat hair. But I've also had a companion, sort of a "white shadow" that follows me from room to room, and someone to complain to when things go wrong. It was often best my thoughtless outbursts fell only on her deaf ears.

"Mer-row-oow" I can hear her calling as she lays the bloody remains of a mouse on the porch step. Having no kittens to feed, she brings to me her catch of the day.

"Thanks a lot, Jo."

As in people, when one sense is missing the others become stronger. Somehow, in spite of being deaf and declawed and wearing a bell, Jo has managed to bring me several "meals" a day for years. She is very sensitive to vibrations. If she sits on the porch with her back to me, I know she can't hear the door open or my voice, so I touch my toe on the floor and she quickly turns and comes in. For many years Jo has known that a shadow crossing her path could be danger.

How do I call a cat that can't hear? It's ten o'clock at

night and I want to go to bed. I stand outside under the yard light where she can see me. Then I wait until **she** decides she's ready to come in, and bounds out from under the bushes in a bouncing run that looks more like a kangaroo than a cat. "Crazy cat," I say, knowing that I'd never get to sleep knowing she was still outside.

When we pull our car into the garage, we see her sitting on the stereo watching us through the window. By the time we enter the house she is already waiting for us in the hallway, ready to rub her white hair against our dark dress slacks.

Jo has given us hours of entertainment chasing the spot of a flashlight, or batting a wad of paper around the dining room floor. When she gets bored, she sits on a kitchen chair, hangs her head way down over the edge, looks underneath, and views me upside down. I guess it's what you call "getting a new slant on life."

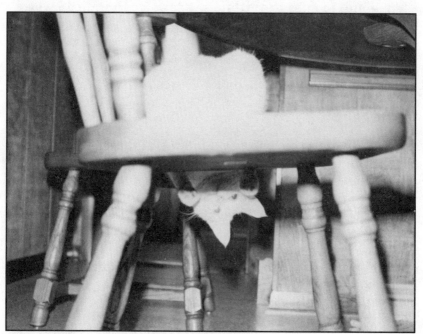

When Jo-Jo gets bored this is her way of "getting a new slant on life."

When Henry lies on the floor for an after-dinner nap, Jo rubs against him and then settles down to sleep next to him, rolling over on her back, front paws together as if in prayer.

Jo-Jo's handicap turned out to be a blessing for her. Instead of fighting for a spot at the tin pan of waste milk in the barn, she gets her own bowl of "Crave," plus bits of fresh fish or chicken she begs for by standing on her hind legs, balancing a front paw against the kitchen cupboard.

Instead of looking for a bit of warmth in the rays of winter sun on a barn sill or against the flank of a cow, she gets to curl up in the pillowed cushion of a rocking chair. Instead of having the calves lick her hide for some sort of petting, she gets plenty of scratching and rubbing from loving hands.

Having survived her neck being snapped by a dog (whose warning growls she couldn't hear), a fever that took days to overcome, as well as numerous tangles with barn cats, she has almost used up her nine lives.

I'm going to miss that white shadow. Her handicap was a blessing for us too!

October, 1988

Double Trouble

It was after ten o'clock that Monday night when I came home from a church meeting. There were two vet trucks parked down by the barn. That's always a bad sign. When a vet calls a partner for help it usually means trouble.

I didn't even go down. They didn't need me, and if Taffy was going to die or lose her calf I didn't want to watch.

Of course I didn't accomplish anything in the house either. My mind was in the barn and my feet kept taking me to the window. Finally the trucks left.

Henry came in. "You have twins to feed."

"Twins! She didn't look that big."

"The second one came backwards, but it's okay. Bill's partner, Joe, was in the area so he stopped by to help."

"How's Taffy?"

"She's up and really crazy for the calves."

All my fears were needless.

86

"We put the calves in the manger because those other two cows in the pen that are ready to calve might accidentally lay on them," Henry said, and then headed for bed.

I was tired and not excited about the idea of changing clothes and wrestling with two new babies. But since it was so important for the calves' lifetime health it had to be done. At no other time would their bodies absorb more antibodies than during the first two hours of life, and no milk has more nutrients and antibodies than the first milk a mother gives. So it was out to the barn for me to feed a bottle by hand, so we knew they got enough.

By the time I got the stored colostrum from the freezer thawed and heated it was eleven o'clock. One calf had already slid under the steel pipe gate and was almost in the gutter behind a row of cows. That would never do. I grabbed her back legs and dragged the slimy dirty little thing back to where her sister slept like dead underneath the grain cart.

At least they were both girls. Most of our twins were one bull and one heifer. Since they share the same blood supply, chances are the heifer will not breed. The cow's nine month pregnancy terminates with small worthless calves and a drained mother.

The men had put these twins on a nice pile of hay, but in trying to stand they didn't stay there very long. Now both were covered with the cow's uneaten silage and lime from the floor. With twine I attempted to tie one to a post of the pen. Even though two of the cows in the pen didn't have their calves yet, they all thought these belonged to them and kept poking their heads into the manger to get at them. Taffy was there too, looking like a skeleton. After being butted a few times by the over-anxious mothers, I erected a barricade of bales.

Putting my fingers in the bigger calf's mouth I was happy to find her instincts working. I slipped in the nipple of the bottle and she sucked—until she felt the pull of the string on her neck. Then she stopped sucking, stiffened, and pulled back. Only an hour old and already rebellious. To keep her from fighting the string, I had to make slack. I hooked my left knee behind her rump, and put both arms alongside her neck to keep her in line and the bottle out in front. This went fine until, feeling a burst of energy or resentment, she thrust her head up sharply. I lost my balance and ended up on my back next to the gutter in the same spot where she had been. "I don't believe this," I said.

No one was listening.

By now the sleeping dead was awake and falling all over in her effort to stand. Smaller and weaker than her rambunctious sister, she could only take a little milk at a time and twisted her head away from the nipple. I urged her to take more. Alternating between the two calves, I finally got about two quarts into each of them.

Next step was to dip their dangling umbilical cords in iodine. I put on a rubber glove so I wouldn't get the brown stain all over my hand. Taking the lid off my little iodine-filled Tupperware container, I held the struggling body of the big one with my left hand and reached around and underneath. One swift kick and the Tupperware went flying, its contents spilling all over the hand without the glove.

I looked and felt like a battle victim. Leaving my charges buried in mounds of straw, I retreated to the house. My clothes reeked of iodine, manure, and blood. I shed them in the garage and headed for the bathtub.

The twins and I weren't done with each other yet. The next morning they got vitamin shots, as well as selenium and iron. A few days later I tried to teach them to drink from a pail. They rebelled again. For some reason calves think they have to "bump" their source of milk, whether it's the cow's udder, a nipple bottle, or a pail. I was soaked again. This time with warm sticky milk.

"Sugar" and "Spice" (guess which one was labeled Spice) were carefully photographed and recorded. They picked up weight quickly. In the next months they would have dew claws, horns, and extra teats removed, and receive vaccines for a host of contagious diseases.

I would tote milk to them twice a day for at least six weeks, as well as expensive calf starter and other grain. They would have hay and water served to them and their beds "made" twice a day and cleaned once or twice a week. What more could you ask?

We ask them to "put it in the pail" two years from now when they become mothers themselves. But please, Sugar and Spice, don't have twins!

May, 1988

Best Friend

"Snoopy . . . Nu-u-u-py . . . Sno-o-py." I called and I called. My eyes searched the jagged line of the hill to the south. I looked west to the road and the woods beyond, and north to the marsh, but the familiar bounding black lab did not come into view. I caught my breath as I heard a dog bark in the distance . . . but no, it was not him.

Snoop dearly loved to hunt. His only fault was sometimes taking off on his own. I had locked him in the garage before dusk the previous night. I didn't want any bow and arrow hunter mistaking him for a running deer. I couldn't forget the dog that came to us last year with an arrow sticking out of his rump like a flag.

Yes, Snoopy loved to hunt, but he also loved to eat. He was never gone long and was always home by feeding time. Now when he did not appear, my heart sank. He was a real pal. Taking his daytime naps by the back door of the house, he sprang to life as soon as he heard it open, and bounced along at your side wherever you went, pushing his head against your leg or under your hand.

In his excitement he would quickly search the yard for something to retrieve for you. Either a stick or the old pair of jeans I had tied in knots for him to play with. He would carry it so proudly, with his head held high, as if it were a prize pheasant. The white blaze on his black chest was as a mark of royalty.

Snoopy followed the tractor for hours when Henry was in the field, and was always at his side in the yard. It was a companion like this that we were looking for when we got the little six-week-old bundle, just two years ago. With our kids gone, we appreciated all the more someone to dote on, and to make the long hours spent outside more interesting.

Once Upon A Farm

When I fed calves, Snoopy was right there, licking off their mouths when they lifted their heads from the pail. Such a gentle dog, he even shared his food with the cats. So affectionate, that sometimes he would just lay his head on you with such pressure, as if he was giving you a hug.

Snoopy was everyone's friend.

Now, sadly, I put his food back in the house. Maybe in the morning he would be there. But morning came, and Snoopy did not. Then I knew something had happened. Did a hunter kidnap him? Or shoot him? I couldn't believe he could get lost. Henry phoned all the neighbors and the radio station. When the feed truck came, he asked the driver to keep an eye out for him. Not a clue. No one had seen a black dog.

Then late in the afternoon one of the other mill drivers phoned to say he had seen a black dog lying on highway 116—dead—alongside a dead opossum. A fast trip in our truck took us to the spot. The highway was empty. No possum, no black dog.

Henry phoned the county highway department. Yes, they

had picked up a dead dog. Did we want the body? It was wearing a red collar and had a white blaze on its chest.

We were a couple of crabby people doing our chores the next few days. Such an eerie quiet in the yard. No one to greet us. For weeks afterwards, whenever I turned the car in the yard I still expected to see the endeared black form rush out to greet me. And yes, tears did fall.

This was the first hunting season that Henry didn't have a dog. He did hear one or two pheasant roosters cackle, and his spirits fell as he thought of Snoopy's joy and expertise at stalking them.

People get condemned for spending money and time on pets. However, it doesn't seem as bad talking to an animal as talking to yourself. Dog food is still cheaper than a psychiatrist.

Not that there is a shortage of dogs. Every year some poor betrayed thing shows up at our farm, usually starved, scared, bruised, and dirty. We always wonder if they were "put off." Some people don't realize the commitment involved in taking on a pet. By making the animal dependent on them, they become responsible for its health and behavior. This means 24 hours a day, 365 days a year—not just at Christmas present time. We never keep the strays. When we make the commitment, we want it to be of our own choosing.

I don't think we'll ever be able to replace Snoopy. But Dixie is trying. She's only two months old, but already a joy. Like Snoopy, she's a cross-bred (they have the most heart). She has learned her way around the barn, jumping across gutters to get to Henry on the other side. Yes, she runs off with gloves and the plastic cat dish, and chewed up Henry's dust mask. She's learning respect for the old cat's clawed swats, but has fun chasing the younger felines.

As I wait for the calf to drink, my arm hangs at my side, dripping milk. Suddenly I feel a soft warm tongue licking my fingers—ah, such bliss.

December, 1987

Escape In Wisconsin

I was struggling to stay awake as our car turned into our driveway. It was after ten. We had taken guests to a Japanese restaurant for supper. The mother, father, brother, and aunt of our former AFS student, Takashi, were as full and sleepy as Henry and I were.

Suddenly I was wide awake. Our headlights spot-lighted beyond the curve of the gravel. A cow! Two cows! They didn't belong there! The group of black and white bodies milling around behind them didn't belong there either.

Their ears went up inquisitively as they turned to look at the light. Alfalfa dangled from Belle's mouth. Her face wore a strange expression of glee.

Henry delivered our passengers in the yard and parked the car at an angle towards the open gate. (It's amazing how gates can open themselves when everyone swears they were shut.)

A large white cow trotted out of the tool shed, boldly running at us. The elder Japanese scampered into the house and spent the next 45 minutes on the inside, peering out.

I ran in for some "workable" shoes and rang Dennis, our herdsman. Several rings told me he was in sound sleep.

"Hello?"

"The cows are out."

"They are." His voice was a mixture of tiredness, disappointment, and disbelief. "Be right there."

In the meantime Takashi, who had spent a year working on this farm with critters like these, knew what to do. Closing the gate to keep in the few unadventurous souls remaining, he hid behind it so he could swing it open when we brought some back.

A lot of bellering was going on at the back end of the feedlot where those "on the inside" saw those "on the outside." They wanted to get out too, but no gate was open over there.

Drunk with the "wine of freedom," our usually docile milking mothers were throwing their heads and kicking hind legs out behind them. One old girl who usually plods into the barn as if she can't take another step, became transformed into a silly young thing with rocking horse motions.

Dennis coming down the driveway, blocked that route of escape. Henry and I plunged into the darkness behind the tool shed and started moving belligerent bodies to the yard. Of course a few ducked into the corn field.

It's lots of fun chasing cows in corn. You can hear 'em but you can't see 'em! You race down a row, the knife-sharp edges of corn leaves slashing at your face. Thinking you have passed the cow you have been running parallel to, you cut across and suddenly come upon her, surprising both of you. She bolts and runs, knocking down more corn than she could ever eat.

Finally managing to bring a group under the yard-light towards the gate, we see them turn aside. What? Oh no! Dear younger brother from Japan wants to help and has stationed himself in front of the gate. He doesn't understand English.

"Takashi! Tell him!"

Takashi tells him the cows won't go through with him there, and we start prodding the wanderers back to the gate again.

Just as I am counting my blessings in that my garden escaped the heavy hooves, I see a shadow moving behind the lilac bush. Yup, she's going down the Hungarian pepper rows, giving them a good pruning. Crossing the lawn she doesn't miss anything, flipping the concrete bird bath with one quick jerk of her head. I move fast when she noses up to my vinca vine flowing out of an ornamental milk can.

After finding a few stragglers between the buildings, we have all the escapees rounded up. They stand in the barn yard looking at us, as if in shock. It will take them a while to settle down.

There must be something about the color of the grass on the other side of the fence—or is it just delight in the forbidden?

September, 1989

The Nest Is Empty

I was overjoyed that day in spring when a pair of wrens moved into the little house I had hung just outside my kitchen window.

The perky brown male flitted around the board structure in the ash tree for days, singing lustily. Finally *she* came and checked it out, going in and out of the tiny opening, hopping on top, even looking under the eaves of the roof; like any good woman, she was making sure it was clean and safe. I imagined her saying, "Seems okay—I like the bird bath nearby, but there was a barn cat prowling around."

When she started carrying in dry grass and twigs, I knew the "little woman" was going to raise her family there.

Meanwhile, in the barn, swallows swooped in and out of the open doors, pasting mud here and there before deciding on the right spot. Finally they selected the ledge of a light fixture, out of reach of the smirking cats snoozing below. This business of choosing a home and raising young was no easy matter!

Weeks pass and the first peeps are barely audible as I walk under the nest. The parent birds make many trips, gliding in and out of the barn doors, working endlessly — filling empty mouths. They become almost fearless in their efforts to care for their young. Such busy, exciting days!

Then, can it be—already? So soon? The babies are out! Looking much like their parents except for bits of fuzz still clinging to their lighter colored tummies, they line up on the wires like kids at a spell down.

Thin voices squeak with demand as the parents bring food, still taking care of their brood even though they have left the nest.

Teetering a bit on the wire, not looking at all confident about being out in the great big world, the youngsters sit tight while the parents jabber a twittering lecture: "Don't sit in any dumb places like you did yesterday, too close to that fat cat! And don't take off until you can get a good start and know where you're going. Get up early and look for food. If you don't move, you'll starve."

Back at the wren house, a tiny head sticks out of the hole. I wonder if these young birds take turns sharing the view, or is one more bold than the rest? Do they have a "middle child syndrome?" Is the "first-hatched" the first one out?

In a few days they are flitting in the bridal wreath bush.

These parents too are nervous about their offspring's initial flight, flying back and forth as they rattle on with scoldings and warnings.

One by one all the youngsters gain strength and wisdom. Then they are gone.

I feel sad.

The parents sit more quietly now. I imagine them saying:

"Maybe we should have built in a different place. The food might have been better."

"I should have been here when the storm struck. Maybe we wouldn't have lost that one."

"Do you think we let them out too soon? Are they strong enough? There are so many dangers . . . ."

Maybe the parents didn't do it all exactly right. But they did the best they could.

August, 1989

P. Wouts-Hanson

Family On The Farm

Kids and Farms

"Watch me catch that cat." Our pint-sized grandson takes off towards the barn at top speed, his short legs windmilling over the gravel.

The tiger kitten is just a youngster herself, but she knows enough to run and easily makes it to the stone barn fence, up and over, away from those grubby little hands that always squeeze her tummy and let her legs dangle.

"She got away." He comes back sadly dragging his feet.

"Should Grandma get a kitty for you?" I walk slowly over to another kitten sitting on the barn door sill, reach down and gently lift her up.

"How cum you can catch 'em, Grandma?"

I try to explain to his young mind the advantages of moving slowly and being gentle.

"E-e-e-e! The werewolf is coming, the werewolf, the werewolf! E-e-e-e!"

I jump and quickly jerk my head to the direction of the screeching sound, first in reflex, and then in true concern over what could be causing such terror.

Dennis' daughter, Lisa, and her friend are running through the hay field. I soon see that the sound is caused by a combination of the girl's own vivid imagination and our lovable, good-natured, black lab. As they reach the soft lawn, drop down and roll in the grass, the dog licks their faces. The screaming goes on in pure delight.

When the grandchildren are here I don't get much accomplished. If I am in the house and they are outside, I keep my ears perked up for trouble sounds. I am constantly running to a window, just as I did when their mother was a child on this place. There are so many things they can get into. One example is when the kitten-chaser tired of hitting the ball, and decided to swing at the low-hanging green apples instead, seeing how far he could send them.

Lisa's three-year-old brother, Donny, is in the question stage. Before you have one answered he is asking another.

"Why do you get to go in the garden?"

"Why are you feeding the calf?"

"Why does the calf have to eat?"

"Why is he hungry?"

Now he is starting to repeat the answers. This gives your brain and your patience time to regroup.

Kids love to spend time on a farm. They like the freedom to run and make noise, to wear what they please, and to actually be expected to get dirty. They experience things first hand, as what it feels like to have a calf suck your fingers, and the realization that "Boy, those cows are really big!" If the timing is right they may even get to see a calf born, and learn a lesson of life.

It's a wonderful place to play hide-n-seek or just plain "run away and hide from the little kids." Imaginations run wild. The big stick on the lawn that no one had time to remove, becomes a black stallion when the five-year-old who was left behind, mounts it and goes for a ride.

There are things to collect like corn kernels shucked off a cob they pulled from the crib, or feathers that have fallen from a fleeing blue-jay. There are bouquets to take to Mom and seed pods to collect. Flowers and weeds are mixed together. To them it is all the same. Beauty is in the eye of the beholder.

The every day chores of the kid that lives on the place, such as scraping the barn platform, feeding calves, or washing the bulk tank, are fascinating at first to a visitor. This interest makes it more fun for the home kid, and even gives him a chance to show off a bit. But after three days it's no longer appealing to either one. Daily jobs are important help to Mom and Dad, however. They must be done, and the kids know it.

If there is a farm pond, it's an exciting place to swim, even if the baby fish nibble on the older girl's legs and send them screaming to their towels. They lay on the grass and watch the swallows skim the water for bugs, and study the fluffy clouds overhead, imagining them to be cotton balls, bubble bath, or lambs. In the quiet peacefulness they bare their souls to each other and dream dreams.

It is my prayer that technology and economic situations do not erase the family farm. Kids need a farm to visit. Some need to grow up there.

Kids and farms grow well together.

July, 1987

Go-fer Woman

I went to town the other day and casually asked Henry if he needed anything.

"Yeah—good, it'll save me a trip," he said, and gave me a scrap of paper which listed the numbers of three sizes of spark plugs. "I'll need a new manila rope for the nose lead. When we clipped that one heifer she tore the old one apart. I don't know if I need one-half or five-eighths inch. Find a nose lead in the store and measure it. Get six or eight feet."

Great, I thought to myself. Also on the list were the measurements for a battery.

"Have them load it for you so you don't get acid all over your clothes. It's for the same tractor they ordered a muffler for. Ask them if the muffler is in yet," directed my busy husband.

"Are there any strengths or anything else I need to know," I asked, recalling past bad experiences when purchasing parts.

"Just tell'em it's for that same tractor, and get the best so it lasts a little longer."

After spending considerable time, I did locate all the spark plugs, and even the rope. I was real proud of myself. Then I asked an attendant for the battery.

"Six volt or 12 volt?" he asked.

I knew immediately I was in trouble. Knowing the tractor didn't help. He said it still could be either voltage. Then he added that it probably was a six volt because it was such an old tractor, and they were out of those anyhow. The impatient expression on his face as much as said, "Why do men

99

send these dumb women to me?"

I phoned home . . . no answer. We have to come back for the muffler anyhow (which wasn't in yet) I reasoned. Then we can get the right one, instead of me dragging that acidy thing back and forth. Right?

Wrong!

Henry was furious, "Why didn't you bring *one* anyhow? You had a fifty-fifty chance. The tractor is in the way of other machinery, right in the middle of the shed. I need a battery *now*."

"Can you push the tractor out of the way?" I meekly suggested.

"Its loader is down." Henry also mumbled something about trying to charge up the old battery as he tromped to the shop. I felt sorry for him and sorry for myself. The "go-fer" ducked into her "hole" until the sun came out again.

May, 1987

Fathers and Sons

"I'm gonna rip that kid up about that. There he goes again, trying to move cattle with the 4-wheeler. I hate those machines—they only make the animals wild and the kids lazy."

The "kid" David Williamson was talking about is in his late twenties, and is David's son and farm partner. Together they raise stud angus and sheep in northern New Zealand.

"Whad'ya think God give ya legs for? Fetch those animals on foot—talk to them—use the dog like I do." David stood watching from a distance, with feet set wide apart, hands hung in fists at the end of taunt arms. His weathered face twisted into lines of disgust and impatience.

"I love them animals and he has no patience with them. Everything's gotta go fast for him. Had to have a new house too, on the land I bought for him. Couldn't fix up the old one that was there. Now he's in trouble trying to pay for it. Well, that's his problem.

"He just doesn't understand. He doesn't know what I've

put into this place. See those fields all cleared and fenced, with the pines, gums, and willows planted for windbreaks? I did that all—by myself—a lot of it while he was off to college.

"I'm 65 years old now and I want the farm to keep going— the way I've always done it; with fence made straight, animals that are well cared for, and plantings of trees to keep the land from slipping away."

David also mentioned that his daughter (who understands animals) is the one who should be farming with him. She had chosen an occupation in a far-away city. David didn't see her very often, which is probably what made her so appealing.

In southern New Zealand, Richard Spencer-Bower looks out over land that his grandfather, as an original settler, bought very cheap. But times are "lean and mean" now. There are no government subsidies and loan rates are 15-18 percent. So Richard is not anxious to invest in every new government "scheme" that comes along. (I like that word they use instead of "program." It's more fitting.)

"One has to weigh it carefully," Richard says, "to see if it justifies the expense, to create volumes of wool and beef that you can't get rid of." He plans on continuing farming the way he has been, with low cost, low labor, "flood" irrigation.

I commented to Richard on the swimming pool in his yard, and the gnarled vine forming a leafy canopy over the veranda of his house.

"I don't ever get a chance to be here and enjoy it," he laments. "We can't afford enough hired help. I'm always out there working," his arm spreads out towards the sheep-dotted pastures, and fields of grain and grass cash crops edged by 40 miles of shelter belts on the 4617 acres.

"Father divided the farm into trusts for us three boys. But what good is that? It has to work as a unit and the wives do not get along. Never did. It's got to come to a head soon."

It was all so familiar. I thought of farmers I knew back home who had worked hard for their own fathers, ever since they were old enough to find their way to the barn. Their youth was spent in long hours of pitching manure, picking rocks, and hauling hay. With that labor came pride in themselves and a respect for life, as well as a keen eye for a good cow and a well-kept field.

Now they are aging and the process of turning over or passing down the farm is not easy—financially or emotionally.

Father-son images form in my head: sons eager to try new things learned in agricultural schools; fathers more conservative and wisened by the labors of life wanting their sons to do, "because I said so." With little margin for error, fathers have trouble finding the patience for the son to learn by doing.

Forgetting his own mistakes, a father may tend to see only the folly of inexperience. It's hard to let go of his domain.

Sons see "old-fashioned" ideas and ideals in the father. "Times have changed," they say, "you have to get with it— get modern." They find it hard to pace themselves and to sacrifice for long-range goals. Some feel it impossible to live up to Father's achievements. There are new and more numerous pressures; outside influences tug at the kids, the wife, and any spare time.

Sometimes it's hard to get priorities in order, for young and old; to know what one really wants out of life—out of living.

For the sake of agriculture in New Zealand, and in America, I pray that fathers, mothers, sons, and daughters find a way to join hands—and shoulders; to give and take; to win respect for their industry; to keep faith.

March, 1991

4-H Ribbons of Memories

Going through a closet I ran across a bundle of fair ribbons. All placings were there, from a paper pink to a satin blue with the entry tags still attached. Memories flooded back to me:

"Mom, who took my cookie?" The freckles stood out as brown accents on my daughter's reddened face.

"O-o-oh," was about all I could say. It was county fair

time. Val had laboriously measured and mixed (under my watchful eye) the peanut butter dough, then rolled and pressed with a fork ever so carefully. When they came out of the oven we picked out the nicest ones. The three that were perfect and uniform were set aside on a paper plate, ready to go to the fair in the afternoon. It was this plate younger brother's hand had raided.

He had problems of his own. Dan had worked for weeks on his junior heifer project. Actually he hadn't started teaching her to lead early enough, so it took "cram" sessions. But she was doing okay, a beautiful black animal with good type and size. The day before he noticed an ugly, grey, scabby splotch on her neck—ringworm! Not serious, but contagious. His dairy leader said he couldn't take her. Such disappointment.

Oldest sister wasn't about to console anyone. She was still sewing the hem in her jumper entry. Then the wool garment still needed careful pressing, and we had to leave in an hour!

After ten minutes of deliberation, another cookie was found that would qualify for the missing spot on the plate. We started to load the car. The cookie-baker went to get her cat for his final grooming.

"Mom! He's not there! Charlie's not anywhere!"

Everyone (except the sewing sister) combed the farm yard, searching the haymow, manger, granary, gardens, and sheds. Charlie was not to be found.

The cookie-thief loaded his wooden desk lamp and found newspaper clinging to the part he had varnished the night before. "Mom! What can I do with it?"

A ten minute session with a turpentined rag and nail file solved that problem—well, at least made it presentable.

Finally we took off—without Charlie. The next morning he appeared at his usual spot next to the cat dish in the barn. I swear there was a smile on his face.

Every year I dreaded entry day for the fair.

Now, looking down at the old faded ribbons that Val had tucked away, I saw that the peanut butter cookies got a third. But the next entry was labeled "Bucky" with the satin blue ribbon still attached. She could always count on her old buck rabbit to come through.

Once Upon A Farm

Older sister's bread, which she had baked ahead and froze, only got a third. But the jumper, as well as the cotton dress and linen suit, earned firsts. Chris loved to sew.

I recalled that Dan got a third on the lamp, but was consoled by a first in dairy showmanship. He was allowed to show a friend's calf in that contest, and celebrated his win by spending his whole allowance gambling on the games on the midway.

Fair time is the climax of the year for a 4-H member. It's competition and reward, preparation and fulfillment, learning and doing, and it's winning and losing.

The 4-H program involves developing skills and knowledge and learning to help others. It is supported by volunteer leaders who donate hours of time and personal resources to teach the youth.

Way at the back of my closet I notice the greying green cover of one of my own old 4-H record books. Opening it to "My 4-H Story, 1954" I read this concluding paragraph:

"4-H has helped make me what I am. I am sure that the four-fold development of Head, Heart, Hands, and Health, through the club program will guarantee many alert and active citizens, eager for progress in our America of the future."

July, 1988

The Stark family when the children were young and growing up on the farm. (back) Lois, Christine, Henry (lower) Valerie, Daniel.

The Stark family with the children as adults, 1991 (back to front) Daniel, Valerie, Christine, Henry, Lois.

Two Little Words

"Maybe I could handle milking twice a day, working a full time job, and even doing laundry, meals, and housework with no help from him—if only he'd let me know he appreciated it," writes a stressed farm wife.

"Thank you" those two little words. Why are they so hard to say? Especially to those who need to hear them the most, members of our own family.

"Well she'd better do it, if she knows what's good for her," I've heard farm men comment. Or, "That's part of farming."

On the other hand, when a man stops working on a tractor to start milking a half hour earlier, so that he can attend his daughter's piano recital (and he hates piano), his wife needs to say, "I know it was an effort for you, I really appreciate it, thanks."

At this time of year we give thanks to God for a lot of things. Not the least of them the fact that our food costs are only 11.8% of our income, the lowest in the world! However this very fact puts a lot of stress on the people producing it.

For them it's a continuing challenge of producing the most you can in the cheapest way possible. The constant juggling of work and time is carried on every day by farm families across the country. The farmstead set among trees and green fields and quiet animals looks so peaceful as you drive by, but within it may be teeming with stress.

For example let me take you through an average day of my diary a few years back when our kids were still home:

Wednesday, August 1, 1973: Danny was up during the night with a sore chest, throat, and eyes—hay fever from the oats. Finished morning milking to discover the steers from across the road were in our yard. We chased them into the barn and then loaded them, a few at a time, and hauled them back. They had lifted a gate off. That will have to be fixed. I went to feed the chickens and in the heifer lot nearby saw a young cow killing her new-born calf. Took the calf in the barn, but it later died. Ran Val into town for her clarinet lesson at 8:20. Then took both girls to a 4-H cooking meeting at 10:00. Picked the cucumbers, made refrigerator pickles and stored the slicers. Then I made spaghetti for dinner.

After dinner I put Dan and Val to work cleaning the old grain out of cow mangers. Helped Chris make bread for the Fair. Then I spent some time helping Henry move the elevator and unload grain. When it started raining I took the tractor to get the gravity box from the field where he was combining. I washed the milk bulk tank. Henry went to work on the tractor that wouldn't shift into high gears. It is constantly on his mind. We need that tractor working and he worries about how much it might cost. His repair work gave him a late start milking, which made him more nervous. Since he had a 7:30 school board meeting, I finished milking and Chris made BLT sandwiches for all of us. Val helps me by letting the cows out and forgets to shut one barn door so we chase two around the yard. Chris goes babysitting. I pull a few weeds in the flower beds and do some laundry. Val and Dan give themselves baths as instructed. I collapse into bed at 10:30. Henry comes in at 11:30. He gives me a peck on the cheek, mumbling, "Thanks for milking tonight." Contented sleep overwhelms me.

Life can be an ongoing process of jumping over stones and stepping around boulders. A few sincere "thank you's" along the way make the path a lot easier.

November, 1989

Strength and Gentleness

Just as I step over the sill of the barn door, a blur of black whizzes past my feet. It's one of the five kittens that are this spring's production of the barn cat department, a solid black, a calico, and three tigers. I stand quietly for a bit and watch as they go running and tumbling in somersaults and chasing tails. The tiger stalks the black from behind a clump of straw. He pounces and has the black on his back, biting him in the neck until he cries. I am just about to intercede when the victim jumps up and runs off in great glee, only to return in a leaping pounce on top of his previous assailant. I go to my work smiling. It's like watching kids at play: sometimes it's better to stay out of it.

Every farmer has had trouble with "that cat disease." With the mattering eyes, diarrhea, and vomiting, they get to be quite scaggy looking before they usually die. It is a viral disease commonly called "cat distemper." It cleaned us out once. Now we vaccinate good mousers that we want to keep.

One of the older cats that fell victim to the disease was a favorite, "Bootsy." We had given her some antibiotic, but she continued to lose weight and finally could not even walk. I'll never forget that day I came in the barn during milking. There was Henry squatting next to Bootsy with her head propped against his leg. His rough calloused hands cradled her face and dispensed antibiotic from an eye dropper into an unresponsive mouth. For ten minutes he worked with her, while his prize cow was being neglected by over-milking as the pulsator pumped away at the empty udder.

"I don't think we can save her," I said quietly.

"But she looked right at me and cried," he said, gently laying her head down.

I was overwhelmed with love for him in his gentleness.

This brings to mind the subject of farm men and animals. Farm men have a macho image of themselves. They are supposed to be rugged and big and tough. But some of the most successful farmers I know have a gentle nature.

There is a quote of W.D. Hoard which I fully support. In a condensed version it says: "Treat all cattle, young and old, with patience and kindness. The giving of milk is a function of Motherhood. Rough treatment lessens the flow. That injures me as well as the cow. Treat each cow as a mother should be treated."

I knew a farm woman with a rascal son who would often disobey and was always playing practical jokes. She was so worried about him getting into serious trouble when he grew up. A friend consoled her saying, "He is always kind to animals. Nothing bad will come of anyone who is kind to animals."

The prophecy came true. He grew up to be a much loved clergyman.

Nothing is so strong as gentleness.
Nothing is so gentle as real strength.
In today's farming the size of your gray matter is more
important than the size of your biceps.

July, 1987

A Youngster Leaves Home

The old white horse trailer that we use to move young
stock bumped up the driveway. I watched it go, eyes peeled
for one last glimpse of the white clover-mark on the black
rump. Henry was taking one of my "babies" away.

Oh, she wasn't a baby anymore, and she wasn't going to
be slaughtered. "Lucky" was going to a new home, to new
people, to new experiences.

Almost like watching your kids go off to college, I mused.
You're happy for them—but yet you miss them. It won't be
the same again. And you worry.

How will they be treated? Cows, like people, seem to pick
on "the new kid on the block." Put a different animal in a
barnyard and she is immediately checked out by inquiring
eyes and noses. She smells different. Some one gives her
a bump to see how she'll act, how much pushing around
she will take. Where will she fit in the barnyard peck
order?

*(How will Jimmy get along with his roommate in college?
Will they be able to share experiences, property, and space—
or will there be a lot of "bumping" going on?)*

It will be strange for Lucky. There will be different fences
and buildings, different food and different people. For a
while she won't know where to go or where not to go. After a
few barbs on her nose and a few jolts from that "hard-to-
see" electric wire, she will be much smarter.

*(Jimmy suddenly finds himself with few fences. He is
finally quite "free" actually. It feels so good at first. But
after running into a few "barbs" and getting "jolted" by
unseen dangers, he realizes he has to set his own
boundaries.)*

109

Will the new owners give Lucky the diet she needs? Don't let her eat too much grain so that she gets too fat, but yet enough to prepare her for producing milk after calving. Will she get the proper vaccines and roughage? She had pneumonia when she was a babe. I hope the stress is not too much for her.

(Who will make Jimmy's favorite foods, such as chicken paprika and poppy seed strudel? He never eats a good breakfast unless someone tells him to. He probably won't wear his cap when it's cold. If he gets sick, his mother won't be there.)

Lucky has always been a little slow on discovering what we want her to do. Afraid to go out of a pen, she's one of those the men actually have to push, inch by inch, their shoulders to her hip to edge her out the door. Will she be put in a stanchion or a tie stall? Maybe a free stall and a parlor will be the arrangement. If she doesn't know what to do right away, will the herdsman be patient?

(Jimmy may not know what courses he wants or needs right away. He will make mistakes. Will his superiors be patient? Will they talk to him—or just prod him out the door?)

The farm that Lucky went to will be classifying in January. How will she do? Will they prepare her properly with conditioning and grooming? I'll be so proud if she rates high. But if not, I know she's still a good animal.

(Semester finals come up in December. Will Jimmy prepare himself properly and not just cram at the last minute? Will he eat and sleep enough through it all? If he does well, I'll be so proud. But if not, I know that he's still a good person.)

Out of sight, out of mind? No. But one has to let go.

October, 1990

Role of the Farm Wife

With my paring knife I cut open the padded package addressed to me. Inside I find a jewelry box containing a gold chain along with a form letter. "In appreciation of the work you wives do keeping records, running errands, and handling customers." It was from the company Henry sells seed for.

"Well," I murmured, "at least someone appreciates me." I shouldn't complain though. Five years ago when my husband filled out that form for his high school reunion, he listed my occupation as "Stark-Acres Dairy—Herd Replacement Engineer." I was glorified! (I feed calves.) This summer he was a little more truthful when he simply filled the space with "her husband's slave."

Seriously, the role of the farm wife can make or break a farm. Companies dealing with farmers today should realize *her* impact on the operation, whether it is physical, intellectual, financial, or emotional.

Nearly 80 percent of farm women are actively involved in managing their family farm business. This can mean deciding whether or not to rent that 20 acres next door, participating in the set-aside, or deciding what bull to use on Matilda.

Most farm women are all too familiar with going for parts and supplies, keeping herd records, and paying bills. Many know how to drive a tractor and operate machinery. A few even put the crops in themselves, do the milking, and then market these products too. They hold their own with "man talk" and the judgmental eyes cast their way.

"When a farm fails," social workers tell us, "it's usually the woman that holds the family together. She buries her pride and does what has to be done."

Many farm women work off the farm, most of them full time. It's hard to juggle that with meals prepared ahead, evening farm chores, the kid's music lessons, housework, and time for each other.

Each family is different and has to decide for itself if the financial rewards are worth the stress and lack of "quality" time. Is it worth it for him to come into an empty house at noon and fix his own dinner? Is she really making that much when the additional expenses of driving, wardrobe, convenience foods, and baby sitting are considered?

Once Upon A Farm

Fortunately for me, my job at a local sewing factory ended when our first child was born. My real career was only getting started. I can relate to young farm women today. I can remember:

* Doing housework at night because the days are spent outside.

* No time off. Working with other family members and part-time help, you sometimes feel you are required to be a saint.

* Getting dirty. Your friends admire your tan, but you hide your broken nails and chapped hands under the table.

I know what it's like:

* Being receptionist. Handling the salesmen by phone or on foot, rerouting them to a better day or a better mood.

* Hosting family dinners and reunions. "Because you have the time and the room."

* Being "Johnny-on-the-spot." Anytime of the day the orders come: "Pull me out." "Go get a belt." "Press the starter for me, it'll only take a minute." "Help me get that heifer in."

* Having dirty boot trails in the kitchen. Being able to tell the season of the year by what crop has uncuffed itself on the stairway steps.

I know:

* You never have a sick husband underfoot, because if he is sick enough to be in, then you are out trying to do his chores.

* You have faith. You have seen God's power in a thunderstorm, and His promise in the sprout of a seed.

* You know what your husband is thinking before he says it. You've worked long hours at his side under all conditions. You understand his feelings.

* That for you, a half hour of private bath time and then cool clean sheets on aching muscles are ultimate luxury.

I know, too, that your greatest and most precious reward is when your husband introduces you, "This is my wife—couldn't do it without her."

March, 1988

One of the many roles of a farm wife is preparing special-occasion family dinners. At the Starks it always included both sets of grandparents.

These Hands

The hands that lie on the clean "Lee" jeans are not used to being idle. The fingers tap the knee and the hands fidget and move restlessly, nervously.

These hands are not old and wrinkled, in need of rest. They are full of strength and life and eagerness. The scars and missing parts are witness to past struggles, haste, and weariness—mute evidence of experience.

The calluses, grease-filled cracks, and broken nails only mean that these hands are not afraid to tackle any task, no matter how dirty, uncomfortable, or endless.

Once Upon A Farm

These hands have been bruised and cut as they wrestled with hammer, wrenches, and welder, twisting and pounding repairs into machinery that tried to be more stubborn than they.

These hands have cradled the slimy head of a new-born calf as they eased it through the birth canal and assisted the miracle of life.

These hands have been stiff and achy from hours of guiding the steering wheel and levers; planting, nurturing, and harvesting the fields they formed and urged into most efficient production.

These hands have pushed a pencil long into the night, balancing income against outgo, calculating which part of the operation most deserved the meager profit.

These hands have carefully measured the few chemicals the crops need to survive, taking care not to destroy the balance of nature in the soil and the wildlife around them.

These hands have folded in prayer asking God's mercy when the wind storm threatened. They have folded each night in thankfulness for health and things accomplished, and then asked continued blessings on their efforts.

Now these hands are waiting in line with others like them. They are going to receive money because their livelihood is gone. They worked long hours each day, but it wasn't enough. Bad weather, bad advice, bad price, bad luck, and heeding the wrong signals have ended it.

Other hands will do their work. Hands that do not really care how good a job they do because it is not their farm. The farm now belongs to some faceless name, in a city miles away. But the name has money to spend and can produce for less, not having to face the resulting abused land and people and towns.

Can these hands be retrained?

Is there honorable work for them?

Or will they become soft and useless?

Will these hands for the first time be doing things strange to them, such as hitting, or holding a daily liquor glass?

For years these hands have been extended in help to others. They guided the halter while showing the neighbor boy how to lead his 4-H calf.

They held the paper that stated the bylaws of the local co-op while serving on a committee trying to keep things under local control.

They put money in the offering plate when it came around each Sunday, as well as pounding a few nails and helping with heavy yard work at the church.

They have even thrown the quilt off the bed at 2:00 a.m. and gone out into the cold when the teenager pounding on the door begged, "Please pull me out of the ditch."

Now these hands are being asked to turn their palms up and request a hand-out. When like so many other hands in this country, farm and city alike, all they really want is the dignity of honest work for honest pay.

January, 1989

Humble Heroes

The young man was slight of stature, neatly dressed in sport coat and tie. He stepped to the microphone to thank those who had honored him as an outstanding Junior Member of the Wisconsin Holstein Association. Then he thanked those who helped him. After mentioning neighbors, teachers, and county agents he said, "Most of all I want to thank my mom. She couldn't come to this banquet tonight because she's home tending the dairy herd. But she kept encouraging me and keeping me going."

It had been only eight months earlier that the youth had lost his father and then took over running the farm as well as attending school full time.

The day before, I had heard another testimony at the women's luncheon of this Wisconsin Holstein Convention. Mary Detloff was Winnebago County's Home Agent about the time I graduated from 4-H in 1955. Now, years later, she was just as petite and dignified as she had been then.

"It's so good to be in Oshkosh again," she said standing at the podium in a neat brown suit, her hair in the same smart cut, only now flecked with gray. Mary had left extension work for marriage and the farm.

Once Upon A Farm

"I remember the day my husband told me to go borrow money to purchase some purebred heifers coming up at the sale barn," she said in a soft voice. "There I sat in the loan office, with a two-year-old on one knee, a ten-month-old on the other, and a wiggly three-year-old seated next to me, wondering why I had to be the one to do this. Little did I know that within a year I would be doing all the borrowing for everything."

Mary's husband died of kidney failure, but Mary kept the farm going. "I had wonderful neighbors," she said. "I could hire good help in the house, but not in the barn. So I milked the 80 cows."

Mingling with other farmers in the hallways, we heard the usual complaints of losing a top cow, or not getting her bred. Things you think only happen to you until you talk to other farmers.

Stories were swapped on how much hay one had to buy this winter and how expensive it was; how cow rations were changed and what it did or didn't do to the fat test.

There were unhappy stories, too, of serious injuries, bankruptcy, and depression. Of the 1300 dairy persons that made "in and out" appearances at the three-day event, many were older people. This caused a good amount of concern.

One older person was Ray Vander Heiden with his perpetual smile that kept his friendly eyes crinkled at the corners, underneath a crown of thinning white hair. Together with his wife, Rosella, and Eugene and Dolly Koch, they co-chaired the event. Having sold their dairy herds they had the time to manage the whole affair with the same adeptness, diligence, and conscientiousness with which they had run their farms.

I heard a baby cry and saw a young farm wife cradling a two week old infant. It was the only way her farm could be represented at the convention banquet. Her husband was home milking.

I took heart in listening to two fine young brothers relate experiences. "You have to spend a lot of time with the cows and pay attention to detail. Even then things go wrong. But we keep working at it," they said. Watching the sparkle in their eyes, determination in their faces, and vibrancy of their bodies as they shifted from foot to foot waiting entrance to a meeting, I realized how much agriculture needs them with all their impatience and strength.

This is the stuff farm folks are made of. These are the humble heroes that make up the two percent of our population, which provides 250 million Americans with food of the highest quality at less percentage of income than any other country in the world.

These are the folks we honor each year in March, during National Agriculture Week. May they be allowed to maintain their dignity. Dignity born of self-respect, dedication, and hard work—the province of the farmer.

March, 1989

P.WOUTS-HANSON

Feeling Nature's Pulse

A Taste Of Summer

Amid March wind and damp cold came a taste of summer. It was good.

One day the mercury in the thermometer broke through invisible bonds and soared to the 70's. The pre-seasonal warmth was like forbidden fruit. I needed to have a taste.

I hang jeans on the washline. They blow freely now, no longer the zombie-like shapes that hung rigid from winter washlines. Behind me I hear a faint crackling noise, like someone shelling peanuts. I peer into the windbreak of pines. No person or animal is there. Suddenly I realize that the unusual early heat and warming sun is forcing the pine cones open. A bit at a time, the points on the tight cones lift and release new life in the form of brown winged seeds.

Walking around the feed lot and down to the ponds, I check the bluebird houses on the way, making sure they are clean and ready for that bird with the flash of heavenly blue.

The red-winged blackbirds and grackles have been back for some time now; but on this walk I hear for the first time the return of my shy friend, the song sparrow, piping out his happy song with a trill at the end.

Two pairs of "rain birds," the killdeer that always cry when rain is imminent, are screaming as they dart about the heifer pasture looking for a nesting place. When the men find their nests of sticks and stones on the ground of a newly worked field, they mark the area and drive around it until the chicks are hatched.

The cows will spend more time outside today. Lunch will be served from the feeder outside, instead of the manger inside. This way they can absorb a little of the sun's vitamin D on their backs, and stretch winter-cramped legs and necks. Some are already lying in the sun, soaking it up.

Our black bear-like dog is still carrying his massive winter coat. The heat is too much for him,and he plunges up to his neck into the water of a nearby ditch, a look of pure bliss on his teddy bear face.

At the old swimming pond's edge I check out the corkscrew willow sapling that my brother gave me. I hoped to use the squiggly branches in floral arrangements, but Henry cut it off twice (accidentally of course) while mowing the pond grass. Fortunately plants, as well as people, with good "root stock" have unbelievable strength and perseverance. The plucky little willow is showing life and new growth once more.

A cardinal is whistling his mating call from the tall trees bordering the marsh. Up above me lovely swans are shaping white etchings on a canvas of blue.

Lois' taste for summer takes her down by the ponds to welcome the birds and the view.

Nearing the barn I pause to watch the tom cat play chasing games with the females in that ancient spring ritual. Dennis' kids are running through the yard, twirling in little circles and falling to the ground, taking delight in being outside without having to wear coats, and feeling the warm breeze comb through their hair.

In the flower bed a patch of green bursting through its grayed straw covering announces that the shasta daisy has made it through the winter.

Under the lawn trees a glimpse of gold formed by fragile aconite blossoms is peeking out from under dead leaves. It surprises me and warms my heart.

Tonight our bedroom window will be open to let in the delightful smell of spring. I wish I could bottle that fragrance of moist earth, fat buds bursting, and freshness in the air.

I feel good to be alive.

On the farm and in our lives there will be days of clouds and rain storms, maybe even some tornadoes, but they won't keep us from remembering and savoring those unexpected days of "summer."

April, 1991

Hillside Renewal

Too long at the books, my body and mind are cramped. I need a walk. Our hillside with its contoured fields and brush-lined fences beckons to me.

Thinking it will be easier walking, I follow a strip of hay field. This is like walking on eggs! In between the little clumps of alfalfa roots, gooshy mud moves beneath my boots like quick-sand. Small sprigs of green are just starting to peek out from the dried up stubble. Each alfalfa root acts like a miniature dam, holding back the water cascading from the plowed field higher up the hill.

A streak of black whizzes past me, as our furry pup races to explore little creatures' winter homes in the brush at the edge of the field.

In the distance semis and cars follow the highway into the hustle and noise of business. But here on my hillside it is still and quiet, as if the land is "sleeping in" and hates to wake up.

The warm rays of the sun nudge the land daily. In a month or so the ground under that clump of trees will be spread with a carpet of wild trillium.

This field ends in a mass of tangled weeds, grasses, and scrubby brush that has grown around piles of stones. The larger rocks date back to our first years on this farm, when we dug under them with shovels and pried them from the flesh of the earth with chains hooked onto tractors. Scads of smaller stones in irregular heaps are the result of sweating aching backs that, over the years, have bent to the task of ridding this hill of its stone "sores."

Following along the edge of the field, I see other foot steps in the mud. The delicate hoof prints tell me why the field doesn't show much green here. The hay is barely out of the ground and already those beautiful four legged thieves, the deer, are robbing us.

Next to a small woods, I stop for a while to let the quiet soak in. A chickadee chants its winter song, "chick-a-dee-dee," soon to be replaced by its whistled mating call. The "rat-a-tat-tat" of a woodpecker echoes from a dead box elder branch.

As I settle myself on a flat rock, an oak leaf drifts across my feet. It had clung to the tree all winter, and now the bursting bud of new life has pushed it off. The cycle continues.

Mother Nature may not be in a hurry, but she always gets there in time. And she knows how to do things right—as long as man doesn't upset her too much. I think about the recent interest in the "natural" and the "organic." There is new value being put on old ways, such as rotating crops instead of pouring on insecticides and fertilizers. Lowly manure is reclaiming recognition as the cheaper and more "land friendly" fertilizer. Chemical farming hasn't satisfied the needs of the hungry or the farmer. Pure food is getting the attention it deserves as people reconsider what constitutes "the good life."

Behind my rock, here and there a few of the more persistent weeds are already poking green heads from under decayed ancestors. Life is taken up again.

The quiet is pierced by the sound of dog barks in the distance. The din changes into brassy honks and I look up to see a crooked V of feathered harbingers. It's a scene of calmness and sureness.

There is something very reassuring about the return of this season, as Mother Nature renews herself—and me as well!

April, 1989

April Air

Henry gets nervous every time he leaves the farm. "Looks like Jim has ten acres planted already. The land is drying."

"It's only April," I say, trying to slow him down.

"Two years ago we had 20 acres of oats in already by the 18th." And he's off to the work shop. The tractors are getting a "physical" and "spring tonic" (oil change) before they're pressed into long hours of service pounding the humpy clods of plowed fields.

On an evening ride we pass a tractor in a field. It's not moving. The back wheels are only half visible above the ground, with the front end looking like it's aiming for a star. Someone had a long frustrating walk home. Someone was a little too anxious.

The next day Henry has a little more patience with the flat tire and the barn repair work that delay him even more.

These warm April evenings are pure joy. The mosquitoes and other flying pests have not yet discovered it's their time to perform. The breezes are calm. No matter where I walk, even along a roadside ditch, everything is green and alive and growing. It reaffirms my faith in God, this order of nature, as I look in amazement at the fern fronds pushing their curled heads through the compressed earth, and welcome back the killdeer and the barn swallows. I contemplate the 16,000 mile flight of the delicate barn swallows, as their iridescent deep blue and rufous bodies swoop in and out of our open barn doors. I always try to leave at least one half-

Once Upon A Farm

door of my calf barn open, even when it is cold, so that they can continue their busy building. They usually return to the same nest site as last year, add a little more mud to the old nest, and start the two or three broods they will raise here before they fly back to Argentina for the winter.

Daylight savings gives us an extra reprieve after milking chores to finish little jobs outside that were pushed aside by the busyness of the day. Like trimming the lawn or repairing that gate latch. It is so calming and peaceful to watch the sun sink away in a bed of rose colored clouds along the horizon. The birds are quiet and the purple martin sentinel standing guard on the corner of his house pops in a hole. I know it is time for me to pop in my house and attack the dishes I neglected all day.

April, 1987

On A Ride

"Why don't you try riding bike?" Henry suggested when long walks aggravated my paining hip.

"My knees will never tolerate that," I said, not anticipating relearning a skill I hadn't practiced since childhood; especially on those bikes with the brakes and the handlebars in the wrong place, gear shifts to worry about, and torture-style seats.

He went ahead and bought used ones for us, then nearly had a heart attack watching me wobble and zigzag. In spite of initial problems, and after purchasing a wider seat—I like it! My hip and my knees like it!

I also like the biker's world of birds, breezing air, scents, and animals. Come, join me:

My favorite route is down our hill to River Road where we go back and forth between the hills. On our left the ditch bank is covered with unruly bushes and small trees, perfect homes for bright yellow goldfinch.

In spring, the sweet smell of white-blossoming elderberry bushes fills our nostrils as we zoom downhill. Later these bushes will hang heavy with delicate purple fruit. Henry's grandma used to make elderberry pie, adding lemon to give the bland fruit a little zing. Only a grandma would have the patience to strip the tiny berries from the fine stems.

Turning right at the end of the road, I think I hear a cat, but not really. It turns out to be a catbird making guttural squeaks and jumping from branch to branch in the wild plum tree. It must have a nest there.

Blackbirds spook us as they jump out of their ditch-side nests when we pass. There are song sparrows and other kinds that I haven't been able to positively identify. Some are very musical.

Just after rounding the curve where the fresh water spring runs constantly, we enter the marsh world of willows and, later in the season, cattails. In spring we may spy a few buttery-yellow marsh marigolds. A robin has a nest in the tall willows and marsh wrens flit about and scold.

At the foot of the hill (where we turn around) is a large willow tree, home of my favorite bird. I call it the "Wichy" bird because of its cheery song, "Wichy-wichy-wichy." This tiny yellow and olive-green bird with a black eye mask is called a yellowthroat. I hear it often, but have seen it only twice.

As our wheels retrace their tracks, a chipmunk scurries out from the grass to the middle of the road, thinks better of it and runs back to the safety of the tall grass.

We pass Wall Street and head west where the bushes thin and there are more wild flowers, graced with butterflies. I don't know all the proper names, but through the summer there have been what resemble delicate white primrose, phlox, pink morning glories, and little blue bells that I would never see from a car. Later on tiger lilies and queen ann's lace contrast with blue chicory and black-eyed susans.

From the small woods on the left a cardinal whistles while young families of white-bellied tree swallows line up on wires as if for inspection. On occasion we are treated to the sight of a pair of cavorting bobolinks, meadowlarks, or cedar waxwings farther up the road.

Turning at the foot of this hill we head back home. Now we have to go up our big hill. (Those gears come in handy after all.) Passing the corn field we see mama, papa, and baby sandhill crane having breakfast. A deer brings her fawn to lunch, compliments of Stark-Acres Dairy Farm. She has the nerve to stand there staring at us with a tender green corn stalk dangling from her mouth.

There are scenes not so beautiful, such as the squashed frog that either leapt too soon or not soon enough; a pile of rotting fuzz that once was an opossum, now crawling with flies; a song sparrow with its feet sticking in the air; and two young raccoons with their insides on the outside. Then there is the garbage, not a lot, but enough chip bags, beverage cans, and plastic-bagged refuse to mar the scene.

Some days I head south across the highway to see Eva Miller's bluebirds or visit the peaceful Nepeuskun cemetery. I chat with Wayne Kaufman as he pulls envelopes from his mailbox.

"Having a good ride?" Wayne asks.

"Sure am, but I always have to go up a hill, no matter which way I go."

"Well," Wayne rationalizes, "then you can come down again."

"Yah, it's like farming—up and down."

"This year we're in a down." Wayne walks to his house, sorting the envelopes and mumbling, "Nothing but bills."

In biking, as well as farming, the trick is to get the most out of your journey without getting knocked off your seat or run over by the "big guys." Struggle up the hills and coast down when you can, tolerating the "road kills" and ugliness, not forgetting to revel in the pleasant scenes.

August, 1991

A Family Overcomes Tragedy

The babies lay on the concrete at my feet, their tiny bodies naked and lifeless. Barn swallows build every year on the supporting ceiling boards of our calf barn (actually a converted old horse barn). The bases of the light bulb receptacles extend just beyond the 2 X 8's to provide a little ledge on which they anchor their mud nests.

But the ledge is not enough support when bales are bounced on the mow floor above. When the resulting vibrations loosened a nest last year, I stapled a plastic sling around it. The plastic became brittle over winter and now allowed the nest to slip out the bottom. The broken mud and crumpled bodies lay at my feet.

The parent birds flew in and out of the doors, bewildered. They sat on a nearby water pipe looking around, then flew out the door again. I felt so badly for them. It was a blue Monday, June 17.

In an effort to help, I scrounged around in the tool shed until I found some old plywood, sawed it in pieces, and then persuaded Dennis to nail them to the boards making nice wide ledges.

The forlorn parents wasted no time crying over disaster. The next morning they started rebuilding quietly, busily, carrying dabs of mud in their mouths. They sat down where the nest was to be and then placed the mortar around them. I wondered how they found mud, since it hadn't rained for two weeks. A pair of swallows has been recorded as making 1200 trips carrying mud to a nest. It's a laborious job.

All day they worked and the nest started to form—but not on my boards. They chose another light fixture farther back in the barn over the calf pen, where part of the thick electric wire coiled beyond the light about an inch or so, forming a better prop. Good choice!

By the next evening the new nest was complete, consisting of three and a half inches of hardened mud, perfectly placed and lined with fine grasses and feathers. Then for two days I didn't see the birds. What happened? I don't know. Maybe they went on a second honeymoon. On Saturday they were both there, jabbering in their liquid twitter, excited and happy once again.

Both birds were in and out every morning. The female would sit on the nest a little while and then leave. She was laying eggs. How did her body know that it had to produce eggs again? I do not always fully comprehend God's wisdom in Nature.

The following Thursday, June 27, exactly ten days after their babies died, the birds were "pregnant" again. They sat

Once Upon A Farm

on the nest. Actually both sexes incubate the eggs, and change places on the nest often during the day.

A week later I needed to fog the barn for flies. Worried that the insecticide might affect the mother's respiratory system, I grabbed a fork handle, chased her out the door and closed it. Ten minutes after fogging I opened it and she immediately sat on the nest.

On July 13, less than a month after the disaster they were parents again. There were only three little heads under the gaping beaks that peeked up every time the parents swooped in with food (every few minutes it seemed). A typical clutch has four or five young, but this was not typical. The parents "dive-bombed" us if we got too close.

On July 31, three teetering babies lined up on the water pipe that runs above the calf pen. I was as thrilled as the bird parents.

The youngsters were fat-looking because of the fuzz still clinging to their necks. They begged with open mouths and cries as the parents fed them. Their little wings beat the air in circles as they struggled to keep their balance.

The next morning they were still there on the water pipe. By noon they found their courage and were gone—but not completely. I often saw them being fed by the parents on the washline or electric wires in the yard. For the swallow parents, as with most human parents, concern does not end when the young leave the nest.

These youngsters now need to become fast and agile fliers, since they feed, drink, and bathe on the wing, and have a long journey ahead of them.

Their diet, which is exclusively flying insects, will disappear when the weather cools. They must fly south, thousands of miles, as far as Argentina and Chile. In order to eat they must fly when and where the insects fly. This means they fly by day and over land, going around the Gulf of Mexico.

When they leave they take summer with them for another year. They'll bring it back next April.

August, 1991

So Long Summer—Welcome Winter

One day the white-bellied purple martins were leisurely sunbathing on power lines. The next day a change in the weather prodded them to serious business, and they were gone.

Unfriendly winds from the north sent migrating warblers in frantic flight. Only sparrows, brassy jays, and a few brave gold finch visit my feeder now. A squirrel scoots up a tree, proudly carrying the cob of corn stolen from the near-by crib. He is in a hurry. Even the leaves seem in a hurry as they tumble and sail across the now limp lawn.

Indian Summer is over. Like a warm friend bidding fare-well, we hate to see it leave. Only the urgency of new tasks prevents us from dwelling on what can't be brought back.

The phone rings. A neighbor's voice says, "I'm running so far behind with silo-filling. My dad's in the hospital again. I had a flat tire this morning. Could Henry bring over the applicator I bought?"

Henry is at the door. "I'm running to town. Broke down with the plow again. Can you help Dennis move those dry cows in? They need to get on better feed."

I'm in the middle of squeezing grapes for juice, and have pails of apples and peppers beckoning to me in the garage . . . but I go.

The cows that had been "exiled" to the heifer lot are happy to return to the grain and silage fed in the barn. As the temperatures drop the cows' appetites pick up. It seems they are always hungry. Their metabolism changes as the hair on their bodies thickens for winter.

All is in preparation for winter as we store food for us and the animals, and secure equipment and buildings for the onslaught of frigid weather. The ground needs to be fer-tilized and tucked in with the plow. End-of-year painting and repairing is finished on barn doors and house windows. It is with a sense of foreboding we fear this sort of dark monster, this thing called winter.

But it shouldn't be. Actually I'm kind of glad the garden is done. Really, I've had my fill of hoeing and harvesting, first wondering if I planted enough, and then what to do with it all. I look forward to taking a bag out of the freezer instead of having to pick, scrub, and cut vegetables.

Somehow, right now it seems simpler to shovel a little snow than to cut lawn every week, and hoe flower beds and water planters.

Long winter chores can be monotonous, but I could use a little routine right now, a day that goes exactly as I plan it. Or a day with absolutely nothing to do except settle down with a good book, or with scrub mop in hand finally find out what's buried in the back of the hall closet.

I might even get reacquainted with my sewing machine. I could do with a day to waste time in the barn, hugging a calf or scratching the neck of that new heifer that is so afraid, or finally holding that cat that always rubs on my legs. Or a day to write letters, or try out that new pot pie recipe that has been shoved back and forth on the kitchen cupboard ever since I cut it out last spring.

I jump in the truck and run the applicator over to the neighbor, thinking ahead to a less hectic season. I wouldn't even mind being snowbound for a day. Winter holds its own rewards, including a beauty and a sense of quietness all its own. I welcome the refreshing change of scene and season.

October, 1989

A Winter Walk

It reminded me of when as a young farm wife, I used a boiled "seven minute frosting" to cover up the lumpiness of my layer cakes. So the new snow had smoothed and filled the angularities of the plowed field, giving it the luscious look of frosted chocolate.

We have had so little snow this winter, I am like a kid out to enjoy it, sliding my boots through the few inches of fluff. So fresh and so clean. A white comforter hiding dead weeds, broken branches, and other debris of winter.

Each branch of drab trees is given new beauty and grace with a frosting of white, seemingly applied with great care.

Even the big bales of old hay look appealing as powder-sugared jelly rolls. (Is it because Henry and I are dieting again that everything appears confectionery?)

Across the waterway the snow has been swept like a sea of foam. My footprints come as a rude intrusion on sacred water. Is this the way the pioneers felt when they broke new paths? Pure exhilaration must have spurred them on.

Ah, but here some footprints betray the early morning activities of others. A rabbit has bounced along the fence and then broken across to snack on a bit of alfalfa under the snow. A little way along the fence a tree has been split by lightning. Its branches have been dropped half to each side, forming a tent. Covered with dried vines, it is a snug hideaway for my furred friend.

I am getting close to the little woods now and follow the hoof prints of deer. They find the easiest way around wild raspberry brambles and through tough undergrowth. It is quiet. So quiet. I am in another world. Away from the phone and the routine, I have escaped here, but cannot escape my inner thoughts or the presence of God.

The woods is unkept with broken old trees lying across each other and young shoots coming up wherever they can. The little animals love it. Here a field mouse left dainty tracks when he came out from under a wild cucumber vine to feast on weed seeds above the snow.

Hoarse calls raise my concern. Crows are noisy, boisterous birds, often cawing loudly to each other. But these are nearly screaming. In front of me a whole flock of the glistening black feathers take to the air in pursuit of a hawk. The blue jays add their shrieks to the din, not really knowing what's going on but always ready to yell about something. Like some people.

The whistling sound of wind on wings turns my head to a group of soft colored mourning doves gliding to an overspreading branch. They are supposed to go south for the winter, but it has been so mild, not all deemed it necessary. Their gentle cooing restores the peace.

Turning north with the morning sun brightly on my back, each snowflake catches a ray and winks it back at me. Some are brighter than others, but all have a pure, simple beauty that man has not been able to duplicate in any expensive engaging ring. It's as if I'm walking in star dust.

The edge of the woods joins a marsh. I am intrigued by many deer prints coming together here. Forming a single trail, they wind through the tall marsh grass, looping around humps and bogs. When we come to the plowed field, the trail becomes much like a beaten cow path.

Memories flood back to me of when as a child I went to the woods for the cows, and put my bare feet on those soft paths, watching the yellow butterflies cluster at the mud holes in the cow lane. Animals are so smart. They must have figured out that as long as we're all traveling the same way, no sense in each one beating down the bushes and thistles. We'll join together and follow each other—makes it easier for everyone.

The trail comes out on an ice covered tractor lane which holds no imprint. I'm sure the deer followed it north to the deeper marsh along the river. But my feet turn south, up the tractor lane towards our barn, the chores, and people problems.

It was good to find respite, being lost for a while in the fantasy world of nature's winter.

March, 1990

P. WOUTS-HANSON

Unpolished Jewels

Julia

"I was almost an April Fool baby," she said whenever we checked the date of her birth. On March 31 she would have been 77 years old. She was no one's fool.

As a child in Yugoslavia she often tended cattle on pasture, standing in fresh cow pies to warm her bare feet. The hardships of farming were not new to her, when after immigrating to Milwaukee and then to the farm, she did the work of both woman and man.

It was Julia who helped pick the stones and work the fields. Machinery made her nervous, but she unloaded the hay, and pitched the silage, and fed the grain. She scraped the walks and washed the udders. If others were late coming in from the fields, she would have the cows fed and in their stanchions, ready for milking.

Julia scrubbed her house and the barn, but her real joy was to be outside. She pulled weeds. A weed whip was too slow for her; it was faster to yank the unattractive intruders out by hand. Quack grass didn't stand a chance with her around. In her zeal Julia torched the steer fence lines (and also half the hayfield one year). Her lawn was scoured with a rake each spring and she kept it trim all summer, sadness lining her face when a drought turned it brown.

"I'll be in the garden," we often heard, as by day Julia planted, hoed, weeded, and picked. At night she put into jars the fruits of her labor: peas, beans, carrots, beets, pickles, peppers, and jams.

Everyone loves to visit the farm. Since the rest of the relatives still lived in Milwaukee, weekend company was a frequent affair. They usually came just before mealtime, and often unexpected and unannounced. Julia would pull some ham or sausage from the freezer, stir up some baking powder biscuits and a cake, and open some of those jars

Once Upon A Farm

from the basement shelves. Somehow she managed to put out a "country dinner" on an hour's notice.

She loved animals. "Draga" (Hungarian for precious) was the term of endearment she attached to all her babies. She mothered calves, pigs, kittens, puppies, chicks, goslings—and our kids. Her charges always came first, as she put aside her own needs to spend time with a sick calf or an unhappy child.

When that child or a hired man forgot to lock a stanchion or feed the steers, she would do it, saying nothing to anyone. Julia kept the peace.

All of this was in addition to working eight to nine hours a day at factory jobs, including many years at Sand-Knit in Berlin, where she also "mothered" other women.

Julia was my mother-in-law. She made lies out of all the jokes connected to that title. I did become angry with her at times, as when she gave up an evening with her friends to do chores for us (and never mentioned her plans). I felt she denied herself too much. But she found her joy in supporting the future of the farm, and the future of her family.

Six years ago this April Julia made her final emigration—this time from earth to heaven. (I know heaven has no weeds.)

Always neat and clean, (with short naturally wavy hair, she was a master of the 10 minute barn-shower-church routine) and not one to be adorned with gaudy threads and paints, or unnecessary ornaments. Julia was a plain looking woman, quiet and self-conscious. Most people passed her by like a piece of rock. Inside that ore was a jewel, its radiance known by those whose lives she touched.

So it is with many people of the land. They are the "unpolished jewels" of the countryside, and the true riches of this country.

March, 1992

City Girl to Farm Bride

Eight years ago she was a city girl holding a job as a spiffy dressed employee. Then she became a farm bride.

"People must think I like cows or something," she said as we sat at her kitchen table admiring the cute cow knick-knacks adorning walls and shelves. "They are all gifts. Actually I'm not a big animal person—but I'm not afraid of them either. There's only one he won't let me milk. You know, I guess I never *ever* pictured myself milking a cow. Now that I'm doing it I have a lot of different feelings towards cows than I ever used to. Like I'm sad when some have to go."

Her day starts at 5:30 a.m. when she goes out to help milk. Even a clean cow in a clean barn can make you a mess, so she wears her "grubs." After morning milking the young family spends a good hour having breakfast together. Father takes time to play with his three small children. Dinner, which usually includes hired help, may not be until 2:00 and supper for Dad at 9:30 when his work day finally ends.

"When the kids nap at 2:30, that's my time to wash the bulk tank and sweep the milkhouse, spray down whatever needs cleaning, and set up for evening milking," the young mother told me. "Then I often do lawn and garden work."

Her work day is long and is spent juggling duties of mother, wife, bookkeeper, receptionist, herdsman, vet assistant, tractor driver, and master gardener. The evenings hold little social life.

When things really get busy, farm women are pressed into service driving tractor.

"I usually rake hay. That saves him a lot of time. I've baled a little, but I get real nervous, afraid I'm going to do something wrong. No, you wouldn't call me a mechanic. Mostly I pick up after him and put his tools back where they belong."

We talked for over an hour about kids and cows, families and farms.

"People just don't understand what you do," she confided. "They say, 'O-o-o-h, you milk cows?' and turn up their noses. But I would much rather have it this way and take care of my own kids. I like being your own boss and having pride in what you accomplish on your own.

"When we were talking about getting married, he said,

Once Upon A Farm

'Farming is a whole different kind of life.' I don't think anyone realizes that until you're actually *there.*"

I was moved by her strength, courage, pride, and energy. Were there any more like her out there?

Yes, I found another jewel in the person of Michele.

It's been five years since Michele became a farm bride. "My father wondered if a city girl like me really knew what I was getting into. My mom can't understand it—that I'm not afraid of the cows," she said.

Since the birth of Michele's three-year-old son, Alex, she doesn't go out for morning milking, but with the new baby, Joel, her day starts at 5:30 anyhow and continues to revolve around the children, her husband, and the cows.

Like the other family, breakfast is together time, to talk and to play. The rest of the day may not be on schedule again. "He says, 'I might be in for lunch,'" Michele complains. "We try to eat supper at 4:30 (before milking) so the kids can eat with us. Sometimes he waddles in at 5:30 saying, 'Just had to get that last load in.' The three meals a day get to me sometimes. There are times I thank the Lord he's not coming home for lunch."

Calves, lawn, garden, and milkhouse chores are all part of Michele's chores, but machinery is not her strong point. "I've raked hay and chisel plowed. Chopping scares me. I ran the combine—once."

"That was the end of that," husband Rick cut in.

The book work, which gets more complicated each year, usually falls to the farm wife. "People just don't realize—farming is a business. I never had any concept of all a farmer has to know. Since I've taken over the books, I've learned a lot."

Both farm wives felt some isolation in their roles. "It's hard, because we don't know any other young couple that's in the same situation, actually working together on the farm. But we're very family orientated. I see my husband, basically, all day. There's not too much you don't know about each other."

Both women are appreciative of parental support, and don't believe a young couple can start farming without it. The hardest thing to accept is, "We always have to be home

for chores. I mean, I feel bad for him. We're at a family reunion and the guys start up a ball game and he has to leave.
Some days I get so depressed. You totally rely on the
weather man and on God. It's like—why do you do it? But—
no, I have no regrets. He's got a lot of hopes and dreams."

June, 1990

A Woman of the Country

"Hey, you can't eat money," Margery said, as we talked
about the cost of butter. "If I'm going to bake, I'm going to
do it right."

Margery knows how to do many things right. One of them
is raising chickens, and Henry's taste for "real" chicken
was the reason for this visit to the small farm she works
with her husband, Norman, on Meadowbrook Road.

"They are a lot of work, and Norm always says I
shouldn't do it anymore, but I like to see the chickens run
around," she says. Her middle-aged body is a lean bundle of
energy clothed in old stretch pants and sweatshirt. It is nonstop movement as the chickens almost "fly" from the scale
to the buckets in our car.

"Let me show you my babies. I was just feeding them
when you came." We cross a graveled driveway but the
stones don't bother Margery's calloused bare feet.

"When I was a kid I had an ankle that turned in. The doctor told my mother the best thing for it was to let me go
barefoot. So it's a habit I've never gotten over but I've never
had any problems with my feet. I stepped on a nail once, but
I just poured a little peroxide on it. It healed."

Getting close to retirement age, Margery's legs were
beginning to bother her from sitting all day at work. "I had
to do something," she said, "so now I ride an exercise bike
three miles in the basement every morning."

We enter the old barn where a beef cow is held in a stanchion while her calf sucks from behind. Margery grabs a
beer bottle filled with oatmeal gruel and cradles the head
of another calf in a nearby pen, which sucks at it like a

confirmed alcoholic.

"We always get a few extra calves to raise, but I don't think that cow has enough milk for more, so I give 'em a little extra. I don't lose many calves.

"I like the farm. I relax by working outside and caring for the animals. It helps me unwind from the stress of my factory job." Feeding out about 20 head of beef each year is a lot of work, but it's not enough to live on, so Margery and Norman have always held factory jobs. They have always known hard work.

Raised on a Princeton area sand farm, Margery milked four or five cows by hand every morning (and again at night) before walking two miles to the Black Creek School. If there was time she also helped clean barns by hand in the morning.

At age 16 she started working for the Ripon Knitting Works sewing "muk-luks" by hand, and has done factory sewing ever since. Married at age 19, her home was blessed with a daughter and son. When Norman's mother had a stroke and his dad lost a leg, Margery cared for them in her home for ten years, with no assistance. It was an order of life set in youth, when she and her sister took turns staying with a sickly grandma, caring for her house, lawn, and garden. Work habits were set early.

"Your job is your job," Margery says. "You do it the best you can, and you're supposed to be there. It's the example my parents set for me. Keep your nose to the grindstone. There's no play until you get that work done, they always told me. Sure we have our problems on the farm, but they have problems in town too. A lot depends on where you're raised, but I like it in the country, where people can't be lookin' down your neck."

Margery's parents also ordered that if anything is happening at church, you are going to be there. "We always went to the Green Lake church, Our Lady of the Lake. And it isn't just going to church and hearin' the word. You just have to be with people and try to help people." Her neighborhood is blessed with this person who is always there to help when there is a need of any kind.

Finding joy and humor in everyday situations, Margery

has organized several mock weddings in the community and is a blonde "spark plug" at celebrations. Her every conversation is accompanied by a warm chuckling laugh.

This too is a precedent set in youth when "fun" was playing ball games with neighborhood kids after chores were finally done. "I loved to play ball. In winter we would go slidin' down snowy hills. Mom would make us hot chocolate milk, and in summer Watkin's cherry flavored drink."

I thought about how kids today don't have to work as Margery did. They say that is an improvement in our society.

Sometimes I wonder.

August, 1990

A Valentine to Farm Wives

The Colby Chamber of Commerce started a contest and program for Farm Wife of the Year back in February of 1970 to honor these dedicated women for their commitment to farm life.

With February being the month of love and hearts and flowers, it's all appropriate. But who cares? Many people do. They just don't make the effort to express it. So are all the farm husbands ordering bouquets for the business partner that is also their wife? No. The only bouquets most farm women get are the ones they grow for themselves when somehow between unloading hay, making dinner, and milking cows they manage to nurture some petunias or zinnias, and protect them from dogs, cats, and wayward heifers.

I really can't complain. My husband brought a dozen red roses to my hospital room when our son was born, and I have received numerous bouquets since (even though he threatens to put atrazine on my house plants).

If you are a farm wife and don't find any posies on your kitchen table tomorrow morning, consider this my "word bouquet" to you.

I am using the language symbols of leaves and flowers found in an old country diary:

Once Upon A Farm

Red Clover for *Industry*—You have worked hard and long; some of you now working off the farm and still coming home to feed calves, cut the lawn, and do housework far into the night.

Chicory for *Frugality*—"Use it over, use it up, or wear it out" is your motto. You wore the coat an extra year and went without new furniture so the farm payment could be made.

Ivy for *Fidelity, Marriage*—You *do* "stand by your man" comforting him when the cow dies, encouraging him when he is down, celebrating with him when the crops are good. He is your partner in living as well as in making a living.

Oak leaves for *Maternal Love*—You are always there for the kids, to wipe a tear, to "talk to Dad about it," to take their turn at milking so they can make that date or ball game.

Wild Daisy means *I will think of it*—You are the one that has to remember where the moisture tester is and when it is time to vaccinate calves. You also remember to get the bills paid on time and to make reservations for that dinner meeting, and don't forget Uncle Charlie's birthday. In your quiet moments you remember the mother and grandmother who walked the paths before you.

Heath is for *Solitude*—There are days you feel isolated, alone, and that no one understands. Yet it is by being alone and doing repetitious chores that you find yourself, who you really are, and what is important to you.

The Shamrock is for *Lightheartedness*—You brush off the cows tramping your garden, or mud tracked in the kitchen during an emergency errand. You keep things in perspective and look for the sunsets, finding beauty in the ordinary.

Ground Laurel for *Perseverance*—You run the errands that keep man and machine going. You soothe and soften the harsh blows that a farm can bring. You are the sounding board and consultant on major decisions, remaining strong in the face of adversity. You are the glue that holds it all together.

A Hawthorn for *Hope*—Your son didn't make the team and the price of milk is dropping. Events swirl around you and you try to remain calm. You cling to your religion and live with the hope of a brighter tomorrow while illuminating today.

The Red Rose means *I love you*—We all love you and "he" does too. It's just that, like all the good things that support life every day, you get taken for granted. When I think of all the great men and women who grew up on farms; all the farm women who cooked for enlarged families during the depression; all those who have given their time to church, school, 4-H, and community services; and how you together with your husband produce enough food for 134 other people, I wonder where this country would be without the farm wife.

The world owes you a bouquet—from the heart.

Happy Valentine's Day!

February, 1992

P. Wouts-Hanson

Old Man Weather

In The Heat

I squat down under Jeannie, one of our better cows, to machine strip her. I keep pushing my head into her belly just ahead of the rear leg that she keeps lifting. She damaged a nerve during calving that affects that leg, so now she limps badly and keeps kicking. It bothers her a lot, but Jeannie has a lot of other problems and so do I.

It must be 100 degrees in between these heaving bovines during a heat wave. Sweat trickles down my nose. Flies are crawling up my legs and biting my ankles. Jeannie has had the diarrhea. While she was lying down she soaked her tail in the stuff. I keep a wary eye on her tail, with one arm ready to protect my face from the makeup I don't enjoy wearing.

Massaging her quarters, I find three are milked out and pliable, but one is very firm. I remove the milker and squirt some milk into my hand. Mastitis. This will have to be treated and so will her uterus. Jeannie calved five days ago, but never passed her afterbirth. The rotting bloody membrane is still deep within her.

All the cows are heaving, some bodies are actually rocking front and back as their lungs overwork in an effort to free the body of excess heat. Jeannie has her tongue extended, hanging outside her mouth, panting like a dog. When I withdraw the thermometer from her rectum I read 106 degrees. Henry and I discuss her problems. We decide to give her the "shotgun treatment," that is hit her all over with everything we have. We administer antibodies and antibiotics into her udder, uterus, and veins. Henry manages to remove most of the afterbirth. My stomach writhes from the horrid smell as I hold the offending tail to one side.

The next day Jeannie seems to feel a little better, eating better, and giving a little more milk. The third day her temp is still 104 degrees. Her eyes are sunken. We call in the vet. He says she may have been all right except for the extreme heat and humidity we have been having. It takes its toll on these huge animals who ideally like it about 55 degrees. Jeannie now is quite dehydrated and also has ketosis. More treatment, more expense, and more of her milk will have to be dumped because of the antibiotics it contains.

The vet asks if I ordered the hot weather. He says cows are dropping like flies all over the country. The least little problem really hits them hard when the weather stresses them this way.

We do what we can for ours. We have large fans going during milking, and more fans in the free stall where they rest. We clean the gutters, barnyard, and free stall every day in an effort to keep flies down. Otherwise it gets too sloppy, because as the temperature goes up so does the cow's consumption of water. A good cow producing 90 pounds of milk per day drinks on the average about 500 pounds of water per day. When the temperature and humidity rise, a lactating cow can drink 10 to 15 times as much water as the amount of milk she produces.

So the hot weather is not only miserable for us and the cows. It also gets to be expensive. The first thing to suffer is milk production, as heat stress takes its toll. There are more vet bills, and the electric bill races with the thermometer in escalation as fans and water pumps run continuously, along with the bulk tank condenser. It works overtime keeping the near perfect food that we extract from these animals at an even cool 38 degrees.

That evening as I pack pickles in jars for winter, I fantasize about canning some of the heat, so I can open a jar in January when I am trying to thaw frozen water pipes for my calves.

July, 1987

Like Caring For A Sick Child

It looked like something burning on the low land. But it

146

was only clouds of dust billowing around Henry as he cultivated corn. Around three o'clock he came up for fuel.

"Look at my back," he said. It was covered with grey grit.
"The tractor is so hot I can't touch the hand clutch. Dust is
so thick I can hardly see where I'm going. I think I'll finish
early in the morning when it won't be so hot."

We don't usually have to cultivate all 70 acres of our corn.
But this year the herbicides didn't work because they need
rain to be activated. The $600 we spent on them could as
well have been thrown into the air along with the dust. The
weeds, especially the velvet leaf, are growing unchecked.
The rotary hoe helped some, but fields that were caked
couldn't tolerate that as the ground broke into chunks,
uprooting the fragile corn seedlings.

One good thing about the dryness, it was good for haying.
No rained-on hay this year. It dried so fast that farmers
were cutting and putting it in the silo right away, with no
curing time needed. Actually it started drying up before
being cut, with the lower leaves turning yellow and falling.
Those that baled hay tried to do it at night, when the over-
heated brittle stems would hopefully not lose all their leaves.
Now the brown stubble sits there, waiting for rain before it
will show vibrant green growth again.

The grain crops have given up on waiting for rain.
They've headed out on short flimsy stems. There won't be
much in the heads. The short stems mean there will also be
a bedding shortage, in addition to a feed shortage next winter. Some wheat has already been chopped green for feed.

Those raising peas and other garden vegetables were
dealt a double whammy—a late frost, and now lack of moisture. Irrigation saves some, but that has its costs too.

Wisconsin is the nation's top producer of peas, snap
beans, and sauerkraut, second in sweet corn, and fifth in
potatoes. Processors ordinarily market vegetables valued at
$600 million. The drought will have no small effect on the
state's economy.

It's like caring for a sick child, this trying to raise crops in
dryness. You do all you can with seed, cultivation, and fertilizer. Then you watch the corn plant bend its head and furl
its leaves, trying to conserve itself. It makes you sick inside.

Once Upon A Farm

A feeling of helplessness overwhelms you. The problem follows you off the farm. It never leaves your mind.

"You never miss the water till the well goes dry," the old saying goes. Yes, the weather is making local and national news. It's also making financial news. Those that make their living gambling with the products of the earth on the future's market of the Chicago Board of Trade are nervous. Prices have jumped as the prospect of rain has dwindled. They don't know how to place their money.

Those that make their living growing those crops are more than nervous. They are depressed. They are hurting.

We have all kinds of chemicals for weed control, very select hybrids for seed, and scientific ways of using them. We have government programs to take acres in and out of production, and to subsidize the export companies so we can control the market. Just when man thinks he's got it all figured out, God takes over and shows He's still in charge.

It's time for everyone to pray for rain.

June, 1988

After The Rain

The sun streams in ribbons of light from behind the clouds. Sunlight hits the drops of rain still clinging to tall weeds on the lawn. The globules sparkle like diamonds. Flowers lift their heads.

Tree leaves brighten up with brighter shades of green. Birds come to life with cheerful song and activity. They dart about after the new supply of worms and insects released by the rain. Barn swallows swoop back and forth, skimming the sea of refreshened grass.

Day lilies lift their heads as if to thank their Creator for the refreshment. The common box elder puts on a new dress of emerald green, and even the drab lilac bush becomes attractive once again. Though its lovely blooms have long gone, the rain glistens each leaf to a rich patent green.

The corn unrolls its leaves and lifts its arms in thanks. The lengths of garden hose that I had dragged from the

petunias by the barn, to the birch tree on the lawn, to the
tomato plants in the garden, lies idle and unimportant
today.

Today it rained!

Cows come out of the free stalls and arch their necks.
Instead of dragging themselves to the barn door, they stand
in scattered groups and let the gentle drops soothe their
feverish backs and cleanse their dust-laden bodies.

It takes a drought of severe nature to bring worthy
attention and appreciation to a basic need of all life.

August, 1988

Weathering The Weatherman

"Drought in 1990?" the February magazine article had
questioned. All winter long the farm media quoted history,
"drought skips a year as in 1934 it came back again in
1936" and predicted dire possibilities, "a cold winter means
a hot summer"—striking fear in the hearts of farmers.

Farmers whose feed bills soared in '88, the year hay fields
turned a dormant brown and leaves of stunted corn curled
into tight rolls.

What a contrast to the recent scene, when wind-whipped
rains rolled across the yard like descending clouds. I knew it
was serious that Saturday night when I saw water running
down the ramp from the upper level barn to join the
overflowing gutters in the lower barn. I padded the calves
with extra straw to keep them above saturated bedding.

"We'll keep the cows in tonight," Henry said. "They won't
eat outside in this weather."

"They'll be swimming by morning," I said. "The gutters
are full now."

We decided to feed them inside. At 11:00 that night he let
them out to find dry beds in the free stall barn. Fortunately,
the rains slowed a little. (We *only* got 3½ inches that night.)
The cows stood for morning milking and Henry and Dennis
hauled away loads of manure and water.

I don't know where birds go when the wind and rain lash

the skies. However, the next morning several very soggy goldfinch perched on the edge of my platform feeder. Wearing quizzical looks, they teetered over two inches of rippling water where sunflower seeds were to be.

"I'm coming, I'm coming," I called to them and went out to clean and fill all the feeders. They ate as if starved.

We were expecting company for dinner. Seeing some ripe tomatoes on the edge of the garden, I stepped in to snatch them for salad. My boot never stopped sinking. I had all I could do to retrieve my foot from the clay-turned-quicksand.

On the lawn I nearly collided with zooming barn swallows skimming over the mosquito-laden grass. They were having a field day! But the sunflower's golden heads sank in mud because shallow root systems couldn't hold them erect. It was the same story with our little patch of sweet corn. It stood at a 10 degree angle with the ground. Henry braved "Alfred Hitchcock type mosquitoes" to retrieve a few ears for our dinner guests.

The rush of water gouged our driveway as it made its way downhill to end up flooding the marsh and fields below. The tile lines will pay for themselves once more.

We don't know what a normal year is anymore. The U.S. has the greatest variety of weather of any country in the world. Seems it's all on our farm! It's 20 below before Christmas and 70 degrees in March. Drought and deluge. Sweat and freeze.

The weatherman isn't much help. He talks about high pressure and low pressure, blaming everything that happened on wayward jet streams, steering winds that didn't steer right, and active fronts that became stagnant.

But there's hope! The National Weather Service recently launched a $2 billion program. With new technology and more highly skilled people it will be able to give earlier warnings of severe weather, with fewer false alarms, resulting in heightened public confidence. (Now there's a need!) In the process I hope they can explain to me the difference between "partly cloudy" and "partly sunny."

Anyhow, the new weather service will be able to give 10 day forecasts. I gotta see it to believe it. The best forecast we have now is to cut hay—then it will rain for sure, in spite of the "partly sunny" forecast.

It'll be nice to know exactly when to cut hay, and whether we should start filling silo with the just-dented corn now, or wait for the corn that might not get ripe? Will the corn even get ripe? That's the million dollar question this year.

I usually fall asleep watching the 10:00 weatherman. He spends five minutes telling me what happened (that I know), and 30 seconds on the "forecast you can remember" which I usually forget next morning when an inch of "partly cloudy" is falling on the ground. How many times we haven't cut hay because of "scattered showers" which must have been scattered clear across the country because the sun is beaming brightly on our *un*cut hay going to seed.

In spite of all the computers, data, analysis, historical research, thousands of man-hours expended, and drought-monger's warnings, it's going to be an "iffy" year.

Try taking that to the bank.

August, 1990

Ice Spells D-A-N-G-E-R!

The large area next to the lilac bush appeared as a mirror on our lawn. It was solid ice. Imprisoned spears of grass stuck up like the bristles on a hair brush as I peered through the glasslike surface. I could see clear to the ground below. I could also envision a bare patch here next spring, as this ice was sealing out all source of oxygen and life to the tiny roots under those greenish blades.

If it was doing that to the lawn, what was it doing to the hayfields? It seemed the weather was taking one last lick at us. After denying moisture for much of the year, now it was sending it in the worst possible form: rain followed by zero temperatures. Fragile alfalfa roots can't take much of that without a protective blanket of snow. With hay supplies already tight, it was not a good situation.

Having this on my mind as I went down to the barn to pay the mill truck driver, I didn't notice the glare ice patch on the driveway. Both feet went forward so fast I didn't have time to put a hand down. Probably was a good thing, because people doing that under the same circumstances ended up breaking wrists and arms.

Anyhow I took the brunt of the fall right on my rump! Then my shoulders hit and finally my head banged against the rocklike ice. The truck driver and Dennis came running, "Are you hurt?"

I was stunned. All my parts moved okay so I jumped up, my head spinning, "I'm okay."

Later in the house my elbow felt wet. Twisting it around, I saw my shirt sleeve soaked with blood. No matter, it would heal. I was just thankful my back was okay. Only bending was painful. Luckily, the fall was cushioned by the thick quilting of my coat, as well as a lot of natural padding I always carry with me.

Our farm is located on the side of a hill, so as it rains and freezes we usually have a toboggan run that starts at our mailbox and ends in the marsh at the foot of the barnyard. Great for our kids' sledding, but dangerous to life and limb.

That afternoon I held my breath as I watched the cows gingerly pick their way across the barnyard. Here and there a clump of manure provided a foothold on the sea of ice. Wanting to escape the biting wind, they tried climbing the slope into the free-stall shed, their hooves slipping and scoring the ice.

A pregnant heifer tried to run and did a repeat of my performance, only landing on her side. She scrambled to her feet and walked away, limping badly.

A neighbor was not so lucky. His cow did the splits, sliding down on her belly with hind legs sticking out in opposite directions. She struggled frantically, as did her owners, in attempts to lift her. They only succeeded in tearing ligaments and damaging joints. The next day the mink ranch got her—for eight dollars.

Two of our older cows were supposed to be in heat, already overdue for breeding. No way were they going to show anything on this ice. They knew better than to try to mount or try any shenanigans with such poor footing underneath.

This would never do. We kept the cows in the barn. With the weatherman promising no immediate change in conditions and visions of the milk truck demolishing the tool shed in a nonstop descent, we ordered a load of sand.

Now the yard looks as if it has cinnamon sprinkled icing. But at least it's a bit safer for woman and beast.

And I have June in January—sand on the kitchen floor!

January, 1989

Getting The Milk Out

"Have you heard anything? Did your milk get picked up?" Our neighbor's anxious voice was loud on the phone.

"No," I answered, "but we still have room for tomorrow morning's milk. Our bulk tank holds 800 gallons."

"Well, I'm full, right to the brim. I start milking at five. I suppose I'll have to dump." His words were full of concern. "My brother said he saw the milk truck in the ditch by Berlin."

Two hours later, at 10:00 p.m. the phone rang again. "This is Mielke, the truck owner. My driver had a little trouble, but we're back on the road. Can you have your yard open by five in the morning? I'm putting two men on the truck. We want to get on the route early so no one has to dump."

"I don't know, we'll try," I said rather doubtfully. As I hung up the phone I looked out at the swirls of white twisting and whirling through the yard. Under the yard light I could see a drift, four feet high, right where the milk truck had to go.

The next morning I was awakened by a growling roar. Crawling out of bed in the darkness, I peered out to see Henry astride his snow-eating monster. He backed the eight foot auger of the tractor blower into the banks, inhaling them and creating his own blizzard with the spray of white coming from the chute, plastering nearby trees and buildings with icy splotches. By 5:00 a.m. a path was cleared for the tandem tank truck.

When it finally arrived at six o'clock, the driver related his terrors of the previous day. He was parked on an incline and pumping milk when the truck started to slide on ice hidden

Once Upon A Farm

under the new snow. It kept right on rolling all the way
down the hill, across a highway, into the ditch. Sloshing,
heavy milk can be a tricky load to haul. It took two wreckers
and hours of work to repair the damage and get him on the
road again. He slept only two hours that night, before going
on the road again.

The mailman may not come, and schools are closed, but
the milk has to get out!

This blast of snow was heavy wet stuff, but at least the
temperature didn't drop out of sight right away. With
modern equipment the plowing went well. Henry and I
talked about years back when all we had for snow removal
was a 9N Ford with a blade on the front. When high banks
on both sides of the driveway drifted full, there was no place
to push any more. The only way to get the milk truck in was
the "arm-strong" method. His mom and dad started at one
end, and he and I at the other. We shoveled the whole 200
yards by hand—never realized it was so long.

*The year the driveway was shoveled using the "arm-strong"
method.*

When farmers meet at the store or the next sales meeting, they will swap stories of their struggles in the snow and cold. It's just one more challenge in the continuous fight against the elements. A water pipe in the milkhouse that freezes and bursts makes a nasty mess. Barn cleaner and manure spreader chains have to be crowbarred from icy bonds. Feed augers and silo unloaders balk as belts slip and brittle metals snap. Always dependable tractors fail to respond just when they are needed most. Doors don't open. When you finally get them chipped and shoveled out, then you can't get them shut again.

One memorable day a few years ago we had all these problems, plus frozen water pipes in the laundry room. When Henry took the four-wheel drive truck through the unplowed crossroad to get thinner fuel for the diesel tractor, its engine stopped. He had to walk into the fury of the blizzard, the half mile back home to get de-icer. When he got to the house I pulled crusts of ice from his eye brows. The barns didn't get cleaned until late that afternoon, just in time to milk again.

We had supper after 8:00 that night. Henry was just dozing off in his chair when the phone rang. Groggily, he picked it up.

"Hi! This is cousin Manny from Milwaukee. I got some extra tickets to a Bucks game. Why don't you come on down? You don't have much to do in winter, do you?"

February, 1988

Winter Is Not All Bad

My "Handy Andy" golden chore gloves were dirty and wet from filling the water tanks in the cold calf barn. Back in the toasty milkhouse I laid them on top of the condenser, still warm from cooling the day's milk. They were almost dry, when I noticed the water wasn't running out of the milkhouse drain. While I was clearing the drain, the condenser fan started up and blew my gloves into the water. I finished feeding with numb fingers.

Once Upon A Farm

No big deal. Just another one of those annoyances that make farming in winter "not so much fun."

Apparel is a problem. In the summer a quick change of shoes and shirt, and I'm ready for the barn. Now I need to pull heavy jeans over long underwear, add three layers on top, plus boots and two scarves to get me through blowing snow or biting cold. When I get to the barn some of it has to come off. It's a comfortable 50 degrees in the barn and about 80 in the milkhouse when the condenser is running to cool the milk.

The men have the same problem. They need long underwear and coveralls to haul feed to steers and young stock that are fed outside, to spread manure, and plow snow. When they come into the barn, some clothes have to come off for milking. Hand and feet movements have to be more nimble than the zombielike creatures they were outside. About the time they get bulky clothing off, some salesman or delivery truck misses the driveway and they can put it all back on and go pull him out.

Even the cows don't think winter is that great. The menu gets quite boring with no green stuff to tantalize taste buds. (Can't even snitch a dandelion over the fence.) They don't mind going outside when the sun shines, and running through new snow like kids let out of school. With tails streaming they push their heads into snow banks and cavort like rocking horses.

But when there's a cold wind coming in the door, it takes a lot of shouting and prodding to get them out. Compare it to trying to chase women away from doors of a store the first hour of a sale.

Then things go wrong. They do in summer too, but somehow it seems worse in winter.

"I came a half hour earlier and still am finishing late," Dennis said one morning. "The silo unloader won't start up. I spent a half hour monkeying around with it. It's all free and fuses aren't blown, but she won't budge." (It's always a "she" when it doesn't work.)

"It could be worse," I said. "You could have had a broken drinking cup." This catastrophe likes to happen when it's coldest, so the barn floor and mangers are filled with water and ice, and the barn cleaner chain frozen solid.

That same day the heifers stood in the yard bellering. "Don't they have enough to eat?" I asked Henry.

"Let's check the fountain," he said, looking at the group standing around the outdoor waterer. The heating element for it was turned on and the dribble of water in the bottom was not frozen, but no water was coming in. The supply pipe coming from the milk house was frozen. It took a day to get that working, while thirsty noses pushed at the floating fountain covers again and again. Some nibbled at snow. Water is not such a problem in summer.

It's usually during a blizzard that your prize cow decides to calve—with problems—and the vet can't get through. Or on the coldest day of the year the spreader chain breaks, and you end up pitching it off by hand. July, even in a 100 degree haymow, looks pretty good about then.

Sickness is more threatening in winter. Calves cough more easily from being confined and inhaling stale air. Like an evil spirit, dysentery works its way through the milking herd, leaving a trail of scours and reduced production. Neither is much of a problem in summer.

But then—when summer comes—the cardinal under the feeder will no longer thrill me every day with his flash of scarlet on white snow.

When summer comes, I forget the excitement of a fresh flower, the comfort of a crackling fire, and the exhilaration of a winter walk.

When summer comes farmers won't have much extra time to converse with their families or each other. This can happen now, even if it is while cleaning the barn, or at a sales meeting.

Winter's not all bad.

January, 1991

Spring Snow

Thick flakes came from the north, like a flannel sheet blanketing the lawn, leaving a green strip of grass running south from each of the larger trees. On the newly seeded oats field it appeared as powdered sugar sprinkled on a chocolate cake.

"Best fertilizer there is," the old timers say.

The birds were confused and taken off guard. They scrambled around at the platform feeder by my kitchen window. Two martins huddled on the south side of their house. I don't know where the others were. There couldn't be any bugs around for them. Maybe they just rested to conserve energy.

Noble heads of daffodil blossoms bent down and cowered like sinful virgins. Chives stuck up through it all, their persistent spikes of green pointing in all directions. Thick tree buds piled high with fluff looked like Christmas tree ornaments. Bits of purple scilla under the lilac bush peek through the snow as plucky little messengers of spring, "This snow won't stop us."

For humans the late snow gives extra time to finish balancing the check book, cleaning the closet, or washing the kitchen walls. Soon the spring sun, warm weather, and pressures of outside work in flower beds, gardens, and fields will make the thought of working inside unthinkable. It will be easily postponed until Mother Nature's next stunt on the weather front.

May, 1990

A Hot Line Faucet

It was already dark when I turned the handle on the outdoor faucet under the kitchen window. The Austrian Pine seedling I had planted was thoroughly soaked. It would take a lot more waterings to nurture its fragile roots and help them grow in the rocky clay soil.

How much watering would my garden need this summer? I wondered as I looked over my little strip of cultivated earth. Two short rows of two-leafed radish seedlings took up their stand in the brown soil, next to the stalwart spikes of onions reaching for the sky. If I could control the weather, maybe I could have a better garden. How much easier farming would be if we had a handle on the weather.

Back in the house, I picked up the bulb catalog to study the brilliant blooms as I settled down in my recliner. Soon the blossoms on the pages blurred and my eyes closed.

I dreamt I was turning the handle on a "hot line faucet." It was a round, spoked handle as big as a steering wheel, painted bright red. My wish came true. I had a "handle" on the weather. Slowly I turned the big wheel to the left. A gentle rain began to fall in the area of Berlin.

The phone rang. "Shut that faucet off!" the caller demanded. "I don't have all my corn in yet. If I don't get that wet spot next to the marsh planted now, I'll never get it."

"But our oats on the hill needs rain to germinate," I protested. "It's coming up uneven."

"Just shut the thing off," he insisted.

I circled the red handle clockwise.

The phone rang again. "I need a little more rain than that," the woman's soft voice begged. "My husband and I just seeded our lawn and planted shrubs. We need a long, slow soak."

Now what to do? "Maybe the day after tomorrow?" I suggested to her, thinking it would give my neighbor time to get his corn in.

"Oh, no, not then. My daughter is getting married. It can't possibly rain on her wedding day! And while I've got you on the line, I don't want any rain the next weekend either. That's graduation, and I'm having all these people coming for a cookout. I just won't have room for them in the house if it rains."

I was about to write her order on the calendar next to the red faucet, but there was an order already written on that day—"RAIN." The conservation club was planting 5,000 trees in a burned-out area far from water. They had ordered rain following the planting to insure the seedlings' survival. Now which was more important?

"I'll see what I can do," I told the woman.

A car pulled into our yard. A tall young man, with the straight kind of face you can't read, got out and strode over

Once Upon A Farm

to me. "Couldn't get you on the phone. I need rain—NOW. Whad'ya shut it off for?"

"Well . . . "

"I've got 10 acres of broccoli seedlings just beggin' for a drink. Turn it on." His face still had no expression. I couldn't tell how angry he was. But I got the feeling he fully expected his order to be carried out.

I started opening the faucet. The phone rang. "Just phoning to make sure it doesn't rain any more today," a deep voice ordered. "We just finished painting all the park benches and playground equipment. You wouldn't want to waste the taxpayer's money, would you?"

"But . . . "

He hung up, assuming his request would be granted.

"Honk! Honk!"

I turned to see two pickups coming down the driveway. A fist was extended out of a window, shaking in my direction. I recognized the stout man behind it as the farmer who bought all those loads of hay this winter. His hayfields, damaged by the winter ice, needed a lot of slow soaking rain if he was going to keep his farm.

The other truck had a contractor's name on the door. I had heard he was behind schedule on his project, and about to lose a sum of money if he didn't get a lot of good weather to finish it on time.

The phone rang again. It rang and rang. The shrill sound vibrated to the very ends of my nerves. I put my hands over my ears . . . and woke up.

I jumped out of my recliner and went to check the faucet. It was small and grey and shut off. I was glad. I didn't want a handle on the weather.

It's not easy to play God.

May, 1989

P. WOUTS-HANSON

Faded Roses

An Old Barn Remembers

Traveling the back roads south of Berlin, we pass a gray, weather worn barn. It's small. Just room for 10 to 12 milk cows, years ago enough to support a family.

Four gaping holes mark where windows once had been, and remnants of side boards stand with jagged edges as if defending their last stand. The roof is gone as well as its previous owners. But what secrets and memories it must hold. What times it must have witnessed.

Such as the day it was born. The whole neighborhood came to share what they had plenty of—muscle power, willingness to work, and hope for the future. The women came with food, and joy at the opportunity to talk to each other.

The barn was the heart of farm life. There were days a man spent more hours there than anywhere else. The sturdy boards and beams anchored in field stone offered comfort and protection and a place to get away. Here and there a pint flask chinked between the stones of the foundation revealed an old man's hidden escape from the "missus."

There were other secrets too. On the north side, out of sight from the house, two young sons had experimented rolling corn silk and sampled their first "smokes," convinced that now they were "men." The feeling lasted most of an hour.

It was in the haymow that a kiss was shared with the neighbor girl who came over to see new kittens. A few years later in the same comforting privacy of the sun dried grasses, he kissed her good-bye and went off to war.

In its bosom the barn cradled kittens, calves, and colts, as well as providing nesting places for swallows, mice, and spiders. The arms of its loft stored food for the creatures within.

Like a main artery running the length of its spine, the hay

track ran across the peak of the ceiling. Horses towed a wagon load of dried hay into position under the opening on the gable end. The fork setter sank the teeth of the big basketlike fork into the loose hay. "Go ahead," he yelled. Horse power at the other end of an attached rope pulled it through a series of pulleys. When the forkful reached the proper spot in the mow, the man up there yelled, "Whoa." The horse driver stopped, the fork was tripped and the hay cascaded into the loft.

My earliest experiences of haying were at about age eight, pulling rope. After the rope was unhooked from the whipple tree behind the horses, I picked up loops of it at about 10 foot intervals and pulled it back to the ground pulley. The whole procedure was repeated until the load was empty. The hardest job, then as now, was packing the hay in place so as not to waste a precious foot of mow space. Let's be honest, there is something richly satisfying in "filling one's barns."

To keep the barn's pulse beating meant not only hauling food in, but hauling waste out. Some folks used a wheel barrow and ran it up a plank to the top of the pile. Others used a manure rail and bucket. The big-as-a-bathtub bucket hung from wheels riding a rail that suspended from the ceiling and ran behind the cows. By means of chains and gears it was lowered to the floor so it was easier to fork and shovel in the mixture of manure, urine, and straw. Pulling on the geared chains raised the bucket, making it easier to shove out the door and be tripped above the pile. Every lad who did the chore can tell of the times it tripped accidentally— before it got out the door. This incident brought words from the mouth that matched what now splattered the floor, walls, and himself.

The barn was often a place to talk and to think. There were many times when a father counseled his son from behind the hulk of an old cow. Both squatted on stools, heads pressed against the warm body that shielded each from the other's eyes. It was easier to talk that way—about how to fix the broken plow, and how to date a girl, and why did Grandpa die? A man did a lot of thinking while sitting under a cow. There were no fans or compressors or radios to make competitive noises, only the twing-twang, twash-twush of streams of milk being squirted into an aluminum pail.

Plain and strong they were, made of sturdy stuff, this barn and its owners. Time takes them both away from us, but their influence remains.

July, 1990

A Place of Learning

The yellow school bus rumbled down our crossroad, covering many country miles. "Catching the bus" has become a part of life for farm kids. Old country schools are closed.

The "powers that be" felt country schools didn't "offer enough." Nevertheless, those humble places of learning hold a warm spot in the hearts of those who parked their feet under those wooden desks. My memories are extra special because the teacher at the squat, white-sided building that I attended, was my mother.

When she applied for the job the old farmer on the school board said, "I'm not hiring any teacher with her own kids in school." Mom, or "Mrs. Luebke," as I was forced to call her, was hired anyhow. My position became much like that of a "preacher's kid." Not only my grades, but also my behavior, were expected to be perfect.

There were no buses. Sometimes I rode with Mom in the old "Model A," but she left too early in the morning and stayed too late, so I usually walked or rode my bike. If the weather was bad and a car couldn't get through the snow, we both walked. Mom was a big woman so I used her body as a shield, keeping it between the wind and me.

Along with the other kids I parked my tin lunch box on a shelf in the long hall and hung my woolen snow pants on a peg. We chattered to each other, going through inner doors to the warm main room.

"I forgot to brush my teeth!" a first grade girl cried. This meant she wouldn't get a colored star on her health chart. Mrs. Luebke not only had to teach health along with curriculum for eight grades, she also was the nurse. It was up to her to apply band-aids and distribute "goiter pills."

"First grade reading," she called, and the little ones left their desks to sit on recitation chairs arranged around a table at the front of the room. Grade by grade we took our turns being called to the front to recite, and receive new assignments in reading, geography, arithmetic, and language.

It took some concentration to do arithmetic problems while the escapades of "Dick and Jane" were being sounded out syllable by syllable up front. A call from Mother Nature prompted me to raise an arm and two fingers.

"You may go," Mrs. Luebke said.

Embarrassed, I quickly went through the back door to the "girls" wooden outhouse attached to the woodshed out back.

Our world expanded by the use of the small brown radio perched on the corner of a library shelf. "Professor Gordon" and his mini-singers taught us catchy songs. I still remember "The Brook" and "Keep Singing."

"Ranger Mac" instilled in us an appreciation of the world around us. With his guidance we went on nature hikes (Mrs. Luebke in physical charge of course) and crammed shelves and scrapbooks with samples of trees, lichens, plants, and animals.

The school was small and crude but the arts did not escape our attention. Miniature art prints were borrowed from the county library, and Mrs. Luebke's diligent reading of the accompanying descriptions gave life and meaning to the artist's work. "Evangeline" by Longfellow became real to us when she half-read and half-acted the poem.

Budding artists were encouraged each week when James Scwalbach shouted "Let's Draw" from the radio, and inspired us to put crayon to paper. Art work was done on newsprint, Mom's effort to save the township's precious tax dollars. The waste of any kind of paper or mutilation of any book was a mortal sin in her eyes.

At Christmas time Mrs. Luebke became choreographer and drama coach. Language classes were turned into rehearsals for the program put on for family and neighbors, complete with a visit from a gift distributing Santa Claus. It was a high point of our year.

No time or talent was wasted. Older, brighter children tutored the slow ones, taking them to the small back room where they prompted reading or flashed times-table cards.

At recess time no one was left out. The less athletic girl was usually chosen last for a softball team—but she was chosen, or else someone would threaten, "I'm gonna tell." Mrs. Luebke didn't tolerate prejudice and tried to give self-worth to the insecure child. For three years she hugged the retarded boy from a family of seven, and listened to him as he stood close to her in urine-soaked overalls, garbling his demands for attention and love.

At the close of school hours we couldn't all rush home. Our list of "duties" hung at the front of the room. There were blackboards to be cleaned, floors to be swept, ashes to be hauled out—coal, wood, and water to be hauled in.

We didn't have school buses, videos, computers, or an AV Center, but we did have the county library, the radio, and a dedicated teacher that made the old country school, in more ways than one, for us a "place of learning."

October, 1989

Mrs. Luebke and her students, including her daughter, Lois (fourth from left in back row). Howlett School, town of Black Wolf, Winnebago County, Wisconsin, 1950.

It Seemed Simpler Then

Looking at our oats turning color, adding summer gold to the varied greens in the fields, I thought about the old movie we had viewed the day before. A home movie of the last time we threshed grain on my home farm.

There was Uncle Charlie Knack on the straw blower. He always wore a big straw hat with the brim turned down, so that as he directed the straw-spewing pipes, the chaff wouldn't come down his neck. That was his job as long as I could remember. It took some skill to construct a strawstack that wouldn't topple over during the next wind storm. Uncle Charlie's strawstacks were works of art.

Charlie's cousin, Hugo, always drove the steamer, and as children we stood with mouths agape when the big black monster chugged its way down our driveway. The "putt-putts" of the steam engine were deafening. We watched spell-bound as the heavy machine inched its way through the yard, leaving lug prints in gravel and grass.

Silhouetted against the sky, lithe tan bodies wielded pitchforks with practiced skill as they caught grain bundles forked up by other men from the shocks below. They stacked them neatly on the hay racks, only to fork them off again when they pulled alongside the separator.

Those not muscular enough to handle the grain were tractor drivers. I was really proud to travel with the crew one year in that important but fun position.

Before that time, my memories are of sinking knee-deep in the grain bin. My cousin and I shoveled the grain from the front of the bin to the back, as men balancing the bulging sacks on their shoulders, dumped in the precious gold. I can still feel the warmth and pickiness of the oats between my bare toes.

There is a view of my dad bringing glasses of liquid refreshment to the men. There were always two things he was sure to have on hand for the threshers, a good supply of coal for the steam engine and a barrel of beer for the men.

From the beer the men head for the house to eat the noon meal, which was another great production. My mom, a neighbor, and I had spent the whole day before baking pies,

making salads, and scrubbing vegetables. Extra boards
were put in the table which was moved into the front room,
not having enough room in the kitchen for the 15 to 20 men.
Special large bowls and platters were brought out.

Smells of hot breads and roasting meats drifted through
the open kitchen windows and screen door, luring the men
in. The kitchen was sweltering with the heat of the extra
bodies and the ovens.

Finally all were served and the last man politely said,
"Thanks, Viola."

We washed dishes until supper time. If we were lucky the
crew would finish our 18 acres of oats that afternoon, and
the next place would "have 'em for supper."

When they were gone our yard returned to quietness. The
chickens came out and scratched in the dust. The kittens
played tag under the hollyhocks. Why did life seem so much
simpler then?

Was the weather more cooperative?

Was there less pressure to "succeed"?

Maybe it was because there were no government
programs.

Or maybe we were just satisfied with less. We found vacation fun at a church ice cream social, and a summer highlight was working and laughing together on threshing day.

July, 1989

The Country Church

I grew up in a country church. St. John's of Nekimi, south
of Oshkosh, and the people that ministered there were not
only my inspiration, but also my extended family. They
were my social life and provided entertainment with humor-
ous readings and plays at the many events held by the
"ladies aid." The annual ice cream social was a highlight of
my summer and I knew I had grown up when I was finally
trusted to handle money and wait on tables. Our Luther
League had Halloween, Christmas, and Valentine parties.
We constructed our own decorations, costumes, food, and

games, as well as devotions. It's amazing we had such a good time—without alcohol.

The church building wasn't much. Heated by a coal-fed space heater, we nearly froze in winter. The boys liked to sit behind the stove where the pastor couldn't see them fool around during the sermon. Coat racks weren't needed because it never got warm enough to take them off. The walls were a no-color wall paper with an angelic border at the top. In summer, bees and flies came through the tilted openings at the bottom of the stained glass windows, providing more distractions for us kids.

Etched in my memory (since the church later burned to the ground) is the life-size statue of Christ above the altar, with arms extended in welcome and love. The minister was an extension of those arms, caring and comforting, yet holding respect with his "law." His time was spent preaching, teaching, and calling. The calls were unannounced in the barn, field, or home, helping out when needed. The little counseling that was needed was done at that time. The people were faithful in attendance and giving of money and service. They were mostly farmers who felt close to God and the earth. Since the country church was the hub of their lives, it spawned many pastors and church leaders.

Times have changed.

Farm numbers have dropped. Families have split. Women work outside the home. More counseling is needed. Stalwart "old faithfuls" have died. Volunteers are hard to get because everyone is too busy. The costs of keeping a preacher and a building have risen considerably, while rural income has not.

Rural parishes have become a "training ground" for beginning clergy or a "holding ground" for near-retirement ministers. In some areas a pastor and full time lay person care for widespread small multiple parishes on a rotational basis. Some ministries are interdenominational. Sometimes different faiths share the same building as a way of cutting costs. Although I am most familiar with the Lutheran church, I understand the problem is universal to all faiths.

The old country church had dedicated pastors who stayed for years. One old saint, the Rev. Robert Girod D.D., served in the rural parish for 45 years, most of them at a two-point parish near Antigo, Wisconsin. He feels that, "Where there are people in the country anxious for the Christian Church and Gospel, the rural church will somehow be there by the grace of God and dedicated pastors. It is a different ball game—but Christ is the same."

One such church is located in the "boonies" of Michigan. Our daughter is a member, and a sometimes Sunday School teacher, superintendent, choir director, pianist, violinist, or youth director. Her mother-in-law writes the monthly newsletter for Leer Lutheran, where about 20 families keep the small Norwegian church going, physically and spiritually. Sometimes they even do their own service when their student pastor (a new one each year) has to be away.

The country church cannot waste time reliving old memories. It lives in the present and is finding new ways to satisfy the spiritual needs of country people.

Its challenge is to help our whole culture to regain its sense of reverence for life—the holiness of land, time, and labor. For these things, and for the country church—We Thank Thee Lord.

November, 1991

The Good Ol' Days

"The only thing I know for sure is that things are changing, and that the changes are happening faster than ever before," the speaker said at a recent dairy meeting. "Just look at the way you feed cows."

He's right about that, I thought to myself. Thirty years ago the dog and I would bring the cows in from a marsh or pasture at milking time. We lured them into the barn with a pound or two of grain.

Now the pasture is brought to the cow! Top quality alfalfa is harvested and served from a wagon or a conveyor belt. The grain isn't just ground corn and oats. It's a complete ration that has been computer tested and balanced. High producing cows may get as much as 35 pounds per day.

Once Upon A Farm

As a girl my daily job was to wash the aluminum strainer and two milk pails in cold water, outside under the pump. Later on we got modern, and I washed two Surge units in the bathtub.

Now our four milking units, as well as the stainless steel pipeline and bulk tank are all washed in place, automatically, and with hotter water and stronger cleaners than my hands could ever stand.

My pa didn't name his cows. He just said, "I got her ma from Knack as a calf. Charlie's old bull sired her." He kept all the neighborhood pedigrees in his head.

Now animals are identified by names, numbers, eartags, and photographs. Records are punched into computers. Printouts not only show you who the calf's great-grandpa was, but also how much milk his daughters across the nation are producing.

When my pa had a cow in heat, he put a rope on her and led her down the road to Uncle Charlie's bull.

Now Henry spends hours studying the records of high pedigree bulls owned by breeding studs. We purchase their frozen semen and store it in nitrogen. We have the likes of ten bulls sitting at 300 degrees below zero, in a canister on our milkhouse floor! "Super cows" are treated with hormones to release multiple eggs. After fertilization the resulting embryos are flushed and frozen, making possible easy shipment all over the world. It's easier than shipping the cow, and any cycling bovine can carry the baby to birth.

My mom used to keep the farm records in a shoe box, and every April burn some midnight oil before the tax deadline.

Now we hire an accountant to decipher complex farm tax laws. He computerizes our monthly records to keep a handle on costs throughout the year.

It used to be if you couldn't do anything else, you could always farm. And if you knew how to work hard you could make it. That won't do it any more.

Today you need to know how to be a veterinarian, accountant, nutritionist, mechanic, agronomist, contractor, zoologist, carpenter, purchasing agent, scientist, marketing analyst, electrician, labor manager, and business manager. If you can't get full training in all these areas, you at least need to know enough to work intelligently with those that possess such knowledge. Oh yeah, you still gotta know how to work hard too.

Coming home from the dairy meeting I go to the barn for chores. Looking down the two rows of cows that I've raised from babies, I notice Princess isn't eating. She looks sick. Now what? It seems there's always one problem or another.

But then, maybe I shouldn't complain. As fast as things are changing with co-op mergers and dairy corporations, cloning and patented genetics, biotechnology and international marketing, and family farms disappearing faster than fresh-baked cookies; 20 years from now these days may be referred to as "the good 'ol days."

August, 1988

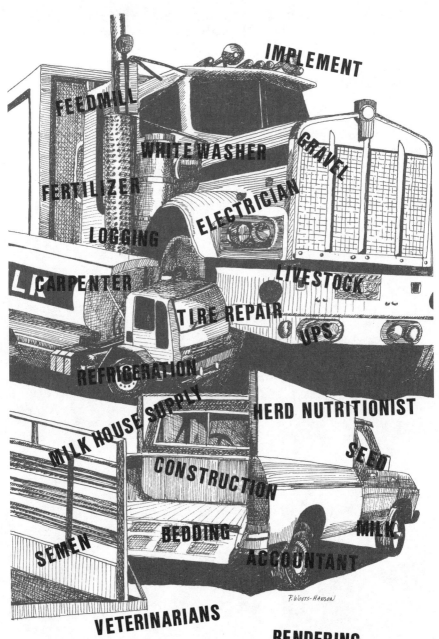

On A Soap Box

When The Trucks Stop Rolling

The feed mill truck backed from the corn crib with a roar and charged up our driveway. It would be back in a few hours with the corn ground and mixed into rations that would feed our 50 cows and 20 calves for a week.

The driveway runs down hill and is washed out from winter wear and recent rains. We need to order some new gravel. It sure gets hard use, I thought, as I watched another truck roll in with a diesel fill for the tank that supplies our tractors. There's also the gasoline truck and the propane truck. My mind started listing all the trucks that regularly roll up and down that driveway.

The milk truck comes every other day to pick up the milk. It's a full time job for him and all the other people that handle that milk on the way to the table.

The veterinarian comes once a month for herd health check (and too many times in-between). We purchase many preventives and treatments from his truck. A semen truck comes monthly to fill the nitrogen tank that holds our supply of "bulls."

Unfortunately, the rendering truck lumbers in like a black monster to "cable on" a cow that didn't survive milk fever or to flip on a baby calf born dead. A stock truck comes for the healthy ones that go to beef market. For the cows that get to stay the nutritionist parks his Ford 150 near the barn once a month. He takes samples of our feed so he can balance their diet. We purchase mineral supplements from him as well as his service.

When a tractor has problems with a big tire, the tire repair service is phoned for an "on the farm" service call. His truck is equipped with everything he needs. The same as the electrician's truck and the refrigeration truck which often come to service problems, or to update wiring, or install new units in the milk house. Cooling 1700 lbs of milk down to 37 degrees in one hour requires expensive equipment to keep working.

Other service people's trucks roll down the drive, such as the barn white-washer who comes every summer, and the carpenter we hire when we can't find time to get a job done or need a new shed.

The guy who has milker soap, boots, milk filters, fly sprays, and everything else needed for barn or milkhouse rolls in regularly; as well as the UPS man and other delivery trucks bringing fertilizer, chemicals, seed corn, bulk supplies of paper towels for cow udders, and a monthly load of sand to bed the cow free stalls—not to mention the gravel truck for the driveway itself.

If prices were better we might see a flatbed truck bring a new tractor or chopper. Money made on the farm gets turned over seven times in the economy. The idea of a farmer making money should not be thought of as a sin. It is an investment in the future of this country. The only flatbed I saw this past year was hauling away old tractors for repair.

This morning our accountant's small pickup rolled down the drive—45 minutes past the appointed time of 9:00 a.m. Phil was late because of two phone calls from farmers searching his advice. What should they do? Should they file bankruptcy? Try to sell? Even a sale now won't cover liabilities plus the income tax on the sale. No one is buying, and yet the farm media lists pages of auctions every week.

"Aw, those farmers are always crying," his city friends tell Phil when he shares his concern.

"But, this time it's serious," he says, "we have gotten rid of most of the rubbish. Now we are losing *good* farmers. They got $10 for their milk in 1978, the same price they are getting now and their expenses have gone up ten times since then."

"What is our cost of producing 100 lbs of milk right now?" Henry asks.

Phil scans the computer printouts of our records and plays a few calculator keys. "$11.10"

"No wonder the $10.50 per hundred milk check isn't going around."

Phil shakes his lowered head, "Something's got to be done. We're not going to have any farmers left. Can't expect young people to take this on. You can't have cheap food and expensive cars."

About 700 distressed Wisconsin farmers dialed the Wisconsin Ag Department Hotline for emergency assistance in January, compared to an average of 142 calls for the month in previous years. Half said recent milk checks were too small to cover basic family living needs after paying loans, service fees, and taxes. Within the past year the farmer's share of retail price has dropped from 51% to less than 40%.

When a farmer like us decides to "throw in the towel" the only thing that thrives is our driveway. It will be in good shape because the trucks won't be rolling up and down anymore.

When those trucks stop rolling—a lot of other things stop rolling too.

May, 1991

Taking A Risk

"My son had his arm around his young wife," the mother said. "I can see it yet. There they stood in the barn staring at the wall. I couldn't imagine what had happened. Hearing me approach, my daughter-in-law turned her face to me. It was white with fear and defeat.

"'Our milk check's . . . no good,' she said. It took all her strength to get the words out, much less believe them."

After talking to this mother, I read the newspaper account of a state legislator's statement, "A suggestion was made that the state buy up promissory notes from the creamery that went broke. This way the farmers get their money right away and the state can wait. The state would be assuming a considerable risk."

Tell me about it.

Tell the farmer about the risk of putting expensive seed and fertilizer into ground that is dry and dusty.

Tell the farmer about the risk of winter ice choking off the already meager supply of hay.

Tell the farmer about the risk of escalating fuel and oil prices just when the tractors go into the spring field work.

Tell the farmer about the risk of taking on a career with no sick days or vacation.

Tell the farmer about the risk of buying land at current prices and then having the value of that land suddenly drop out of sight.

Tell the farmer about the risk of sending milk to processors for a month for them to use and sell, before he gets paid or even knows how much he will be paid.

Tell the farmer about the risk of putting in a corn crop, not knowing what the market price will be six months later.

Tell the farmer about the risk of paying high prices for beef calves, gambling on a good price when they are ready for market 18 months later.

Tell the farmer about risking his body and mind in a most stressful and dangerous job.

The farmer knows about risk.

But does the state?

Can the state risk more empty farmsteads? More unpaid taxes? More cuts in school funding?

Can the state risk knocking down these few remaining brave souls who are willing to work 12 to 14 hours a day for $2 an hour just for the pride of ownership?

Can the state risk losing more young farmers that are consumers and citizens in rural communities?

Can the state risk having absentee landowners buy up land and run it without commitment or care?

To chance losing more good farmers would be the greatest risk of all. The state must get its act together on financial security and not put the farmer at the end of the line.

We need that young man with his arm around his wife. Just how badly we haven't even fully realized yet. But I guarantee you, they are worth the risk.

Our state, and our country, can't risk not having them on the farm.

May, 1989

Nightmare—The USDA Ran Our Farm

What most farmers knew all along, the GAO (Government Accounting Office) has finally investigated and put into print:

The structure and management practices of the USDA (United States Department of Agriculture) have been largely unchanged since the 1930's. The archaic agency has become a massive and expensive bureaucracy which does not meet the needs of the nation's largest industry, agribusiness. During the 1980's while the farm population fell 34 percent, the number of USDA employees rose 24 percent.

The charges are:

*Inefficiency of structure

*Near-sightedness—fails to plan in advance

*Too much spent on overhead (more than on the benefits given out in some counties)

*Exclusively production oriented—neglecting global marketing, effects of biotechnology, water quality, and food safety

*Has become a revolving door for special interest groups

I read this news clip just before going to bed. It affected this dream:

Henry was replaced by a director of the Dairy Division of the USDA. Our farm had been selected as a "proving ground." The government was tired of telling us what to do. Now it was going to show us.

The first thing Mr. Director did was hire two more people. "We need one person to keep track of government regulations on CRP, wetlands, ARP, tax implications, SCS, pesticide rules, and FHA loans."

"Not a bad idea," I said, thinking about how many hours Henry spent reading up on this stuff in his "off" hours.

The person was a "she" that Mr. Director owed a favor. He built her a new office on that three-acre piece west of the house. Then he had it landscaped with full-grown trees.

The other new employee was a relief milker for Dennis. Mr. Director said, "It's ridiculous that he puts in so many hours in the barn. No one in my office works those kind of hours."

I didn't have much argument for that either, except I was wondering how this was all going to fit in the budget. I guess that doesn't bother government people.

On Monday Henry and Dennis were repairing and cleaning the round baler before storing it for winter. Mr. Director stopped them. "Don't waste time on that now. We won't need it until next summer."

"It could be rusted up by then, or we might have to wait for a part," Henry countered.

"Then we'll buy a new one. I have a buddy who owns a John Deere plant. He could use a little business."

One day Mr. Director announced he was going to Green Bay to purchase feed concentrate in bulk. "They have a good price up there for big customers."

"But don't you think we should support the small towns around us?" I asked.

"Small towns—who needs them? We will be adding 50 more cows to qualify as a customer for this importer."

"We will what?"

"Fifty more cows. They'll be here Monday."

"Where are we going to put them? If you crowd them we'll have disease problems. What records do these cows have? Who picked them out?"

"Haven't seen them. I know a guy who works for the UW-Madison research lab. He says they are a deal. A cow is a cow."

Some deal. Within two weeks our herd production dropped in half. We were all working twice as much and administering more antibiotics than this farm had seen in years.

Another day I went to town and passed the crib at Jim and Bonnie Michaels which we rented and filled with surplus corn. It was empty! I questioned Mr. Director.

"Oh, I sold it. I hate to pay storage costs."

Hoping to enlighten him, I invited him to the statewide tele-conference on milk marketing issues.

"Marketing, huh? I haven't much experience in that. Congress just tells us to produce. By the way, I ordered twice as much fertilizer for next year. We'll need more chemicals too. Have to get more feed for those extra cows. We'll be taking out your contour strips so we can get in there with bigger machinery."

"But the government helped us put them in! Do you realize what that will do to the land?"

"Should be a super crop for at least one year. After that I'll be moving on to another farm to whip it in shape."

I woke up to what I dreamt was the auctioneer's gavel. It was only a blue jay cracking seeds on the wooden feeder outside the window.

Government reports do not make good late night reading.

November, 1991

Aldo Would Have Loved LISA

He died before she was born. But Aldo Leopold, guardian of the land, would have recognized LISA as his own "love child." LISA, low-input sustainable agriculture, is the name given to old ideas with new importance and new ways of putting them in practice.

It used to be called "conservation" when we were kids in 4-H, writing essays and giving speeches on "Hawks and Owls Should be Protected" and "Contour Plowing Can Save Your Hill."

Now it is called LISA, also referred to as "sustainable" or "alternative" farming. Basically it means using technology and management instead of high amounts of chemicals and fertilizers, while maintaining or improving production. LISA's methods of crop rotation, cultivating, contouring, and "green" fertilizers have been around for a long time, but were viewed as old fashioned or low-producing. Now in light of a shortage of water, pure air, and top soil, people are taking a new look at her. They're taking low chemical input seriously. LISA's coming of age.

The price crunch and drought had a lot to do with it. (God works in mysterious ways.) When farmers cut back on chemicals because they simply could not afford them, many found out it didn't affect production all that much. During the drought herbicides didn't work and farmers ended up riding the cultivator anyhow, rediscovering that it is effective, cheaper, and safer. (It's something the big farms don't have the labor to do.)

Most of the criticism of chemical farming came from the farmers themselves, as the following quotes prove:

"I pretty much grew up on the river. Being here, I always wanted to make sure it stayed in good shape."

"I think we should leave the place a little bit better than we found it."

"I switched to low chemical input when my father died of throat cancer."

So a number of farmers did their own experiments, often in spite of opposition from government and industry experts. The results were amazing! Soil fertility actually rose after several years of no bagged fertilizer.

Here at Stark Acres, Henry himself vowed off of some products when he took instruction for his pesticide applicator's license. He learned that if you walked into some sweet corn fields within two days after application, you would not walk out again. He has always preferred rotation to pesticides and is considering cutbacks on atrazine.

Wisconsin's sustainable agriculture program was started in 1987 with $2 million. The money was taken from penalties paid by oil companies that violated pricing regulations during the 1970's. Most effective use is made of the money by tapping that great resource—the creative imagination and practical ideas of farmers. They apply for funds to develop farm labs, shops, machines, and computer programs, seeking new methods using plant nitrogen, cover crops, soil and manure tests, crop scouting, and other methods right on their own land. "The best fertilizer is the footsteps of the man who owns the land."

The Aldo Leopold Center for Sustainable Agriculture in Ames, Iowa will fund its future on farm research with a tax on fertilizers and oil products.

A different twist is that, unlike most girls, LISA likes worms. Experimenters are redeveloping an appreciation for them, finding that earthworms are nature's link to healthy soil as they move nutrients and improve soil structure.

But LISA has some enemies too. Lack of information, influence of chemical companies, low prices, and government programs are stunting LISA's growth.

Technology is a necessary part of our future, but it must be intelligently conceived and carefully implemented. It's time to slow down this runaway horse that has been galloping full speed towards the cliff. Put a bit in his mouth and reins in our hands, so we can determine where we are headed. Land-use ethics are still governed by economic self-interest.

Areas that profit from sustainable agriculture are the farmer, the land, the water, and the future of our children. I mean, after all, let's get our priorities straight.

Aldo is watching over LISA. In his own words, "Our bigger-and-better society is so obsessed with its own economic health as to have lost the capacity to remain healthy."

February, 1990

P. Wouts-Hanson

Passing The Torch

The Family Farm Is Changing

I looked at the yellowed newspaper clipping we found in the wall. I couldn't believe it! It was written in 1928. Way back then? And by a Berlin area farmer too.

Ira Mitchell said, "I find it pays better to keep what cows can be properly fed and cared for, rather than a large number not so well cared for. I also believe in crop rotation and practice it as much as possible. I believe in diversified farming for this particular locality, as we never have a failure of everything."

Well—now we've come full circle. That was basic common sense then in 1928—and it still is.

In between then and now a lot of economists' recommendations have come and gone. Consider the blue silos put where they should not have been, high lysine corn, corn on corn on corn, fancy feed additives, and insecticides urged into use and then prohibited. We were told to get bigger. Now we are told that maybe that wasn't such a good idea. We should get better first.

We were told to specialize. Now we are told to diversify. We were told to pour on fertilizer. Now we are told to cut back. The latest is to use bovine growth hormone, and to do it quickly (before the resulting milk flush lowers prices once more) or we'll be the losers.

Now I'm not against progress. It's brought us a lot of wonderful things such as the milk pipeline, hybrid corns, improved genetics, and advanced machinery technology.

But the end result of the farm crisis is that many of the young progressive farmers, doing everything right in someone else's eyes, have gone out of business. Producers have been made to feel as though they must adapt to high-tech practices to be successful.

Today's farmer has to be a rational decision maker. He is

no longer the dummy who is lectured to and told how to do things. He has to realize that what the university says may or may not work, and adapt those things that make sense for his operation.

It all boils down to basic laws. Only God can create. What you take out of the land you have to put back in. To get something out of a cow you have to put something in, remembering she is a ruminant animal. No one has changed that yet.

Change. No one likes it. The older you get the less you like it.

How many of us have had a grandpa on the farm? How many of our greatest leaders grew up on a farm where they learned determination, honesty, self-respect, hard work, stamina, and responsibility?

But things don't look good for the family farm.

In its efforts to keep food cheap, the government has manipulated farmers' prices lower than they have been in a decade. Americans pay 12% of their disposable income for food, Europeans pay 27%. What were once proud industrious farmers have been reduced to "wards of the state." The 1986 government payments of $29 billion in farm subsidies accounted for nearly all of the net farm income.

Food production will be kept up. By technology, subsidies, foreign investment, or whatever it takes. But as it always is with change, you sacrifice some to gain some. In the changing of farm life structure we are sacrificing a valuable training ground for future citizens. It's an intangible by-product of the farm that can't be replaced.

April, 1988

Pass It On?

I ran into Shirley at the farm supply store. We had been in 4-H together, but I hadn't seen her for years.

"Still milking?" I asked.

"Well yeah, what else?"

"Do you have a son in with you?" I felt foolish asking. For sure one of their children would be taking over the farm.

Shirley's pleasant face changed to a look of impatience and sarcasm. "No, we have four sons and none of 'em have shown any inclination to buy the place. I'm getting tired. We're too young to retire, and too old to handle it all ourselves."

I knew exactly how she felt. So do a lot of other aging farmers. There is a quiet rebellion going on in the peaceful countryside. Young farmers are not following in their father's footsteps. The strange thing about it is that most parents are glad they're not.

Cycles repeat themselves in agriculture, but this has never happened before. High school ag classes are reduced to almost nothing and even omitted in some schools. Colleges of Agriculture, even short courses, are begging for enrollments.

Some young men start out in partnership with their fathers, and then begin to wonder about the huge investment of cash, time, body, mind, and soul required to make it go.

Henry as a boy, with his father who repaired most of the machinery himself.

Once Upon A Farm

They are torn. For many, their heart wants to keep the family farm going with all the familiar objects and traditions. But they look around and see that investing all that capital, education, time, and energy in some other venture would give a much better pay back. The current prediction of lower prices for milk, grain, and beef doesn't give them a lot of incentive.

Oh, they know about the satisfaction of independence and the pride of ownership connected to farming. But when you are already under a cow when the sun comes up, and too busy and tired to see the sun go down, it really doesn't matter much.

They know that when you never get a day off or even a milking off; when you are snoring in the chair as soon as your last mouthful of supper slides into your belly—it may be hard to hold a marriage together.

For others, it's in their blood. For them nothing can compare to working with the turn of the seasons, the challenge and response of caring for animals, and the freedom of self-scheduling (which like all freedoms requires self-discipline).

What worked in the past isn't good enough anymore. Farming can't be just a way of life. It's not something you dabble in. You have to be committed.

The young man that "goes for it" knows that in addition to the unknown weather perils he always faces, there are the hazards of a whimsical government. He knows the profit margin is small; that he will have to study management and marketing and finance. He realizes that he may not have the option of owning all his own land or equipment. He would like to have his wife work alongside him, but she may have to work off the farm, to help support it.

It's a weighty matter. I don't envy the young people of today. But the older folk don't know exactly what to do either.

And yet there are still rewards there. It's an honest job and an important job. There is a closeness to nature, to life and death, and to God, not experienced in many other places. It's still the best place to raise a family. It's an occupation where you see with your own eyes the clear-cut results of what you do with your own mind and your own hands.

December, 1987

Henry's mom and dad say good-bye as he leaves for U.W. Farm Short Course. Henry farmed in partnership with his father for 12 years.

Grey Land

"Sometimes I wonder why we still do this?" Henry said. His hand was across the small of his back as he stiffly climbed the hall steps. The men had pushed hard to get the corn in. There were the usual problems such as a broken sprayer, miscalculation of fertilizer, and a monitor that wouldn't work. It was early in the season yet, but like most farmers we don't trust the weather, and have learned to "make hay when the sun shines."

We know our working days are numbered. Who will run our land? A neighbor? Will it become weeds? Or overrun by hunters and recreation people?

It has become a part of us. The blue clay down below that *has* to be fall plowed, even with its underground network of drain tiles. Those tiles were put in a bit at a time, over the years, as we could afford it. The first three miles were laid 30 years ago. Henry unloaded each 12 inch cylinder of cement, by hand, from a flatbed wagon and placed them on the ground next to the tiling machine.

At the time we had only an old SC and DC Case for tractors. It took them both chained together to plow sod on blue clay. Any woman who's ever driven a tractor on the end of a chain will appreciate all that my abused ears heard by the end of the day.

Henry knows the land like the back of his hand, including where the sink holes are (they have claimed more than one hired man: "I wanted to see how close I could get"), and the odd shapes and sizes of the strips on the hill. "The neighbors thought we were nuts," Henry muses. "When we cut the hill into ribbon strips, they wondered how we would ever work it." Yet the strip cropping stopped the gouging and runoff that had been washing away precious top soil.

There is no blue clay on the hill—there are stones. The ravines at the edges are lined with walls of rocks. They've been piled there by our hands, the hands of our parents and kids, and the hands of Paul and Bill, Alan and Inert, and Gary and Ron and Kevin, and about a dozen more young men who, over the years, have supplemented muscle and income on these fields.

In one corner there's a bit of woods, untouched by machine or beast, where the trillium cover the virgin soil with a white carpet each May. The bordering marshes are worthless as farm land, but invaluable to wildlife. We know where you can walk through, and where you won't make it. I smile as I think about the young man who after sinking a tractor on a fence line said, "I couldn't walk through it so I took the tractor." We needed two wreckers and a 20-foot cable to retrieve it.

Yes, we know our land. As yet, it has not been abused by negligence or raped by overproduction. But what lies ahead? There are 300 million acres of this "grey land" that is owned by persons near or in retirement age. How does it get transferred to a new generation?

The northeast states are paying their family farmers high prices for farm development rights. These states want to keep their land in farming. Why?

"People are beginning to recognize the non-renewable resource that we have," state officials say. "Good farm land is worth protecting."

"It's just good business sense to take care of your Number One industry," says a senator from Pennsylvania.

Twenty-four percent of the jobs in Wisconsin, directly or indirectly, depend on agriculture. Europe believes the well-being of a nation's farmers is tied to the well-being of the nation as a whole. Agricultural programs command a huge percent of their federal budget. A leader says, "It is a mistake to become dependent on outside sources of food."

Technology is pushing us to get bigger. One half of the food in the U.S. today is produced by four percent of the farmers. History has proven that concentration of land ownership leads to oppression, poverty, hunger, and eventually revolution.

I've always wondered why the government is so concerned about how many cars we're selling or how many homes we're building; and yet blindly continue to use and abuse our greatest natural resource, the land and the people that work it.

May, 1988

Dispersing The Herd

The cows were beautiful, with black and white coats gleaming, tails washed and fluffed. One by one a leadsman brought them into the sawdust arena of the sale barn.

Their owners, Bob and Fran, sat high in the stands, their hearts in their throats. Their dairy herd was the object of around-the-clock labor for the last thirty-some years. Now it was being sold.

The habits and the dispositions of each animal were as

Once Upon A Farm

well known to them as those of their own four children. These bovines and their predecessors had not only provided a living for those four children, but also taught lasting lessons in responsibility, discipline, and pride.

Bob's eyes roved around the bleachers, which were only half-filled with prospective buyers. He was disheartened by the small crowd. With low milk prices, more people were selling cows than buying them.

"It really doesn't matter," I offered, "if the ones there are 'bidders' and not just 'gawkers.'" There were young and old, shabby and neat, many wearing farm caps and jackets with a variety of logos, some cowboy boots and tennis shoes amongst the work shoes. Some carried canes, and some carried babies, some faces expressing eagerness, others skepticism.

"Here she is if you want instant milk to fill your bulk tank," the auctioneer bellered from behind his podium at the back of the ring. "Calved 2 ½ months ago and milking 95 pounds a day. Take her home and put her to work for you."

The next cow entering the ring had a perfect white question mark emblazoned on a black head, the dot ending up exactly on her nose. "We named her 'Question,'" Fran said with a smile. I knew Fran enjoyed naming calves as much as I did.

"She's light on her left quarter—or heavy on the right quarter, however you want it, but that's the way she sells," announced the man with the gavel. The sale barn staff had been milking the herd for four days, so they were aware of any problems. Both they and Bob did their best to present the animals honestly. However, not all buyers realize that a cow's production may drop considerably when she is put into a new situation, with different feeds, unfamiliar people, unusual procedures, and strange housing. The day was as traumatic for their animals as it was for Bob and Fran.

Bob almost seemed more interested in who the buyers were than how much. His words spoken weeks ago came back to me, "I just hope they go to good homes."

An old couple, frail and grey, bought five animals. "I hope they're not for themselves," Fran said. "Those people are too old to be milking."

"Perhaps for a son or grandson," I said hopefully. "Sometimes the old eye is still a little wiser."

"Here comes Bob's pet," Fran said as Contour-A Minnie entered the ring. Almost all of the animals carried the "Contour Acres" prefix. As the sale catalog proudly advertised, "A Homebred Herd, with regular herd health program including calfhood and cattle vaccinations, a low somatic cell count, and Feb. 1991 DHI Rolling Herd Average— 20,352M, 3.7% 756F."

"There's Baby Dot, we let her run all over the barn when she was little. She was naughty. Now when she sees you coming, she goes the other way."

Fran waved to a young woman coming in past the food stand at the side of the room. It was their daughter who had taken off work to be there. Later I found out that after being there five minutes, she left. "She always walks through the barn when she comes home for a visit," Fran said. "The boys help out a lot too." To watch the life work of her family be put through the ring like so many sacks of grain was more than the farm daughter could bear to watch.

"Did Bob sleep last night?" I asked Fran.

"We haven't slept for the last four nights—ever since they went on the truck last Saturday. That was the worst. It's better now that it's almost over. The last month has been terrible—wondering if you did the right thing."

At the beginning of the sale the auctioneer had announced the statistics of the sale and the reason for selling, "Bob needs foot surgery and the hired man wants to go farming on his own, so Fran and Bob made the decision to disperse."

"More like Fran made the decision," Fran said with all the heaviness of that decision in her voice. But to watch her husband suffer unbearable pain in his foot and knee was an unacceptable alternative. It was also Fran who arranged the following four-day trip to Nashville, leaving at 2:00 the next morning.

"You are too young to quit milking," people told Bob.

"Yeah, but I've been doing it since I was twelve years old."

The day—a year ago now—was not without hope and

optimism. After purchasing several of the cattle, a young farmer said with a laugh, "My hired man quit yesterday, and here I am buying cattle!"

Bob and Fran would return from Nashville to plant their 500 acres to cash crops and feed for the 110 steers and young heifers remaining on the farm. Spring is a season of hope.

To survive would require a conservative lifestyle, a good amount of hard work, wise management and practicality, as well as appreciating the pure joys of life such as family (a first grandchild was due soon) and nature (Bob planned to start a field of wildflowers).

They may have dispersed the milking herd, but the memories and the qualities that enabled them to develop that herd remain.

April, 1992

A Vanishing Breed

White whiskers jutted out like stick pins from his wrinkled chin and grey eyes peered up at me from under jagged eyebrows. The old farmer had come to us last spring for drought insurance, necessary in order to collect government payment for the previous year's drought.

He shuffled into our family room, his back bent at a permanent forty-five degree angle. The pungent smell of Ben-Gay exuded from the white back brace strapped over his flannel shirt. "I never thought I'd see the day we had all these papers to fill out," he complained. "I dunno. Sometimes I wish I'd gone out of it when I still felt better. But you know it ain't easy to give it all up . . . all you ever had. It ain't much, but it kinda becomes a part of you. Why is that? Then what would I do?" His voice rambled on in low tones, coming from deep within as if he had no control over it. "I talked to some guys that sold—said it was the worst thing they ever did. You just keep going as best you can."

Henry started filling out the form. "Do you know your social security number?"

The question prompted a frantic search through the baggy pockets of his overalls. Thick thumbs struggled through the cards in his wallet. "Here's my medicare. Gotta have that too now, you know. Can't find it. Ma must have it some place at home."

Henry continued apologetically. "The form requires that I ask you these questions. Are you or do you intend to go bankrupt?"

"Huh!" he chuckled low, "Pretty close to it, but not yet."

A phone call to his wife and his signature completed the paper work. As he left and literally crawled into his battered old truck, I thought about how he and his wife and a few neighbor kids kept his few animals and small farm going. Or did the farm keep him going?

He was one of a dying breed. Weaned at an early age onto raw hard work, they grew up learning to pinch pennies and appreciate neighbors. They were not much for keeping up their wardrobe, or government programs, and didn't like wasting money, salesmen, or doing housework. They did appreciate good food and plenty of it, a good sermon, as well as a good talk with anyone. And they always found time for talk, in spite of spending three weeks husking a field of corn by hand. (It's a job that now takes one hour by modern picker, and farmers don't have time to talk to each other.)

This breed usually managed to know everyone else's business as well as their own. They rated a man on honesty, how hard he worked, and how much he gave to the church.

Recently we greeted another of this hearty stock.

Lean, wind-burned, with eyes that crinkled at the corners and sparkled with energy, he came to buy seed for the sixty plus acres of corn he still plants and harvests.

"I'm 80 years old," Elmer said proudly.

"You look good," I said, and then immediately regretted the pat phrase, remembering the joke that stated there are three ages to a man's life: young, middle, and "gee, you look good."

He accepted it anyhow and said, "Don't feel worth nuthin' lately. Got that flu, can't get over it. Don't like it when I can't work."

We stood in the front room looking out our picture window

at the farms beyond the marsh, on the hill, and over by the river. We talked about who used to live where and who wasn't farming anymore.

"I know this place," Elmer said with fond remembering. "Used to have meals in this house when I worked threshin' crews and with silo fillers as a kid. I hired out on a farm near here."

"You worked hard at a young age," Henry complimented.

"Sure did. You got boys?"

"Not on the farm."

"Yah, that's the way it is lots of places now." Elmer's voice trailed off as he gazed out of the window. "So many of the boys can't stay on the farm no more."

Sadness tinged his voice, as if he was saying good-bye to something.

Indeed he was.

January, 1990

Auction Day

The weather was as unpredictable as farming itself that March day. The wind whipped out of the west. Temperatures dropped 20 degrees from the 50's the day before. Bits of snow riding on the winds reminded us that winter wasn't done with us yet.

Around eleven o'clock, pickup trucks were coming up our crossroad. I didn't recognize many of them. Why so many? Then I remembered. Our neighbor was having an auction.

At one o'clock we put on snowmobile suits, warm boots, and lined gloves. Parking our truck in our adjacent field, we walked past the rows of trucks all pointed to the auction farmyard. There weren't many new fancy trucks. Most had beaten tail gates and muddied or manured sides, evidence of their services on the farm.

Walking down the driveway, we passed the skeletal barn with its insides long deserted by man and beast. Disease had robbed the owner of his youth and the ability to pursue the career he loved. Bob had long ago sold the milk cows.

His knees wouldn't bend anymore. He kept fat steers for a while—a reason to keep going—something to do with all the corn he grew. Now they too were gone.

Behind the barn the auctioneer sat in his truck throne. The side windows were propped open under the camper top. From there he had visibility, but yet protection from the wind. His voice over the loudspeaker system boomed throughout the yard. "Let's get started with this fine box of necessities." He knew his trade well, starting with the junk to give the late-comers a chance to get there. Didn't want to miss any possible bidders on the big items.

In spite of the bad weather there were many farmers, all sizes and shapes. Good used machinery was hard to find. There were canes and crutches and old farmers with their young sons towering above them. The sons' faces were eager and bright, the fathers' tired and full of concern. Most of the men were in their 50's or more, just curious to see "what it went for." A used machinery dealer was there to get an idea of prices. If he found a bargain he would try to resell it at a higher price.

The machinery was strung out along the top of a hayfield. Reminded me of hanging out all my underwear on washday, for everyone to see.

Farmers crawled under the self-unloading wagons to get a better look at the working parts. They climbed on the tractors, kicked tires, and wiggled moving parts. There aren't any guarantees with auction purchases. When auctioneer Don Wagner bellers, "Sold!" it's yours—no exchanges, no refunds.

"We got two wagons here. You can buy 'em both or one at a time. Who'll give me four—gim-e-four-gim-e-four . . . " the big man's chant went on. Its beat sometimes excites a man to bid beyond his desires—or common sense.

"Sold to the man in the yellow cap! What's your number? He only wants one wagon. That means we got the best one left."

The more stubborn man sets a price in his head and won't go beyond it. A disk we could use was up to $1800. "I got 18, who'll give me 19?"

With a tilt of his head, Henry's bid was in. At $2100 he

Once Upon A Farm

said, "That's it," and turned around.

The auctioneer's man watching for bids came up behind him, "Want to try it once more at 2150?"

"Nope, thanks." Henry's mind was made up. The other bidder got it for $2100.

The auction truck rolled down the line. Bob trailed behind in a pickup driven by his brother. With his head down, his eyes seemed to be far away. It was as if he didn't really want to see this, but couldn't stay away either. Had to see who came—how many—how much. Didn't really like to see everyone swarming all over his field, trampling the little alfalfa seedlings, climbing on his machinery, poking and probing around.

Bits of conversation floated to his ears. "I got those two feeders for $350. Thought that was pretty good."

"Wa-hl, looks like they fed a lot of cattle already."

One by one the trucks hooked onto their purchases. Having what they wanted, they didn't wait until the sale was over, just settled with the bookkeeper, and were gone. By the time the sale was over, half the machinery was gone.

Bob watched the green chopper go. He had prepared a lot of meals for his "girls" with that. The new corn planter, with its bright yellow fertilizer buckets and tottering row-markers bounced down the driveway.

I sensed Bob's feeling of the blood draining out of his body. It wasn't easy to let go.

Hopefully, "the torch is passed," and other young hands will tend the machines with the same care, raising crops and animals the way Bob loved so much.

March, 1989

Twilight

For The Sake of The Farm

Mornings while the baby napped
She washed up the milk things,
   and fed the calves from the pail.
The milk inspector might come
   and she must not fail;
For the sake of the farm, you know?

After serving dinner to the hungry men, she said,
"Well Babe, out to the field for you and me.
I will drive and you will ride."
The crop must come in today
   while quality is at its peak;
For the sake of the farm, you know?

After evening milking and supper,
Now was her time . . . yes, her time
To do the laundry and scrub the floor,
Mend the overalls and paint the door.
The best hours were given to land and animals;
For the sake of the farm, you know?

He was in a hurry when he jumped off the wagon,
And didn't see the fork lying with its tines upturned.
Deep into the sole of his foot it went.
A trip to the hospital and then back to the tractor,
The work must go on;
For the sake of the farm, you know?

Out of bed at two a.m.
That young heifer needed help calving.
Together with the new mother they struggled and pulled,
Then slapped new life into the wet little thing.

Once Upon A Farm

Back to bed, with a good feeling—another life saved;
For the sake of the farm, you know?

When the children were a little older
    they took their turns,
Cleaning the barn, milking the cows,
Working the fields, putting hay in the mow.
Sometimes they gave up good times and friends,
But it had to be done;
For the sake of the farm, you know?

Any money spent had to bring a return;
So a new car was sacrificed for a bulk milk cooler,
Fancy furniture was forfeited for new cow stanchions,
A vacation trip gave way to tiling the low land
    where the hay froze out last year;
For the sake of the farm, you know?

The farm prospered and grew, the children did too.
Mom and Dad had their dreams . . .
Perhaps taking a child in business with them.
With youth and experience and knowledge,
What a winning combination it would be;
For the sake of the farm, you know?

But one daughter married and moved far away.
The second was lured by the city and the things it offered.
The boy said, "I'll work with my mind,
    and not with my body."
And so the parents carried on alone;
For the sake of the farm, you know?

There were other young men that wanted to farm,
But the money was just not there for two families.
The government said,
"You have been too efficient, you have produced too much!
Some of you have to leave—the profit must be cut!"
But they stayed anyway;
For the sake of the farm, you know?

Oh, they could sell to hunters or sportsmen
Or city people looking for a spot of beauty.
But to cut the place in pieces,
    and leave the barn stand empty?
And the fields go to weeds?
It just wouldn't seem right;
For the sake of the farm, you know?

His back is weak,
His step is slow,
She longs for time to read and sew.
But they want to stay and make it go;
For the sake of the farm, you know?

September, 1984

The Lilac Bush

It was already an old bush when the newlyweds parked a
house trailer next to it, 36 years ago. The space between the
lilac bush and the sun porch of the farm home was neatly
filled by the 27 foot, old trailer.

The lilac bush waved its out-reaching branches benignly,
when a year later a baby girl filled the small trailer with
happiness.

The crooked branches nearly prostrated themselves when
tornadic spring winds tore at the lilac's leaves and rocked
the little trailer. The anxious young father rolled his precious child in a protecting carpet grabbed from the floor,
and the little family ran to the safety of the farm house
basement.

The sun did shine again, and the lilac bush saw the little
girl playing on the lawn. She was often accompanied by a
big collie dog and the grandmother in old slacks and
kerchief.

The following year the trailer disappeared. The little girl's
face frequently appeared at an upstairs window of the
house. In place of the trailer sat a big tractor tire filled with
sand, and some pipes that supported two swings and a slide.

Once Upon A Farm

There was a nice green picnic table too, often surrounded by family and friends.

Behind the lilac, in the earth of the garden, the grandfather helped the little girl plant apple and pear tree saplings. He wanted her to always have fresh fruit.

In a few years, two more little children joined their older sister on the lawn in play. As the children grew older, the parents often joined them for an evening game of softball. The lilac was proud to extend a long branch to serve as "first base."

At the edge of the lawn the driveway ran past old tool sheds, corn cribs, and a chicken coop, down to the barn, and then formed a loop on its return. An old grey Ford pickup, a well-worn Chevy station wagon, a 9N Ford tractor, and SC Case, as well as bicycles and coaster wagons ran their wheels over the gravel.

The lilac transformed itself each spring into a sweet-smelling bouquet of delicate lavender sprigs. A few branches would rot or break and fall away. They were always replaced by eager new shoots. The lilac remained, unchanging.

Its feet were covered with weeds and stones where the lawnmower didn't reach. Sometimes the girl would escape there to her own secluded haven. She piled the stones into neat rows and formations, as she created future dreams.

Things were changing on the hillside beyond the driveway. Machines came to form grass waterways and strips of fields that wound their way around the hill, hanging onto its precious thin soil.

The children grew. The lilac witnessed driving lessons as the old straight-stick pickup bounced around the hay field and was "parked" between trunks of tall box elders at the lawn's edge.

Age and heavy snows took down the old sheds. They were replaced with poles and steel, much more serviceable, but not nearly as charming. A new workshop replaced the old garage. Lights from the shop fell on the leaves of the lilac late into the night, as the grandpa and his son worked to lift an engine or wrench an old combine or wagon back into service once more. A gas tank was tucked underground (where it was safe they said) and topped off with a tall pump wearing a glass crown hat.

Spring storms, winter ice, and summer sun came and went, year after year. Only the lilac remained the same.

The children are gone now. The lilac only sees them on rare occasions. Those grown children replaced the pipe swing set with a lovely wooden one designed for older people. The grandparents are not seen anymore. The lilac misses hearing the grandpa's whistling, and the grandma's bustling body in the garden nearby. The little saplings are now huge trees, laden with fruit each fall. They remember their promise.

The mother now has time to give the lilac some attention. She has replaced the weeds at its feet with daylilies and phlox. Its arms are filled with birds that come to lunch at feeders hanging from its branches.

The old sun porch of the house has been replaced with a family room, and a bow window frames the lilac when the mother and father sit inside, observing the seasons come and go.

The gas tank was taken out of its "safe" resting place, when authorities reversed their advice. The wooden slatted corn crib has been replaced by domed structures of cold wire. The barn, its yard, and free stalls have been extended to provide room for the extra cows needed to keep the place going.

More machines and bigger vehicles, faster and more powerful, rush up and down the driveway. But the drivers appear less happy than the whistling grandpa on the 9N Ford.

New people and different children are in the yard and on the lawn. Only the lilac remains the same.

July, 1992

Return To The Home Place

The sun had already disappeared behind the woods as I stopped my car under the cottonwood tree in the familiar

Once Upon A Farm

farmyard. The remaining light was without shadow. Its eerie glow gave the place a different look. I got out of the car and stood there. It was so quiet. Nothing moved, not even the cottonwood branches. There were no birds around—no one was feeding them anymore. Even the stray cats had deserted the place. There were no longer any crops stored there to attract mice.

A shiver ran through me as I unlocked the warped old door. It needed repair. So did almost everything else around here. It seemed as if the whole place was dying. My father was dying too.

He had outlived his body which now lay prostrate in a nursing home bed. His beloved farm was up for sale to provide payment to the people that regulated input and output of that body. I was here to remove personal belongings, before the auctioneer's troops took over.

Inside the long rambling house the rooms were even more quiet. I hastened through them out onto the front porch. My eyes surveyed the tall poplar trees bordering the lawn. Below them a few brambled rose bushes were all that remained of what was once Mom's flower garden. The rickety barn, with clapboards missing, looked like a toothless old man. The half-doors hung crooked. Like Pa, it had seen its best days.

Inside the barn it was dark and empty. In my memory I could still see the twelve milk cows held in small wooden stanchions. Between them and the horse barn was an alley for the loose hay Pa threw down from the mow above. It was here I spent hours cuddling baby kittens and watching a newborn calf discover life.

Crunching sounds from the horse mangers behind the wall betrayed Pa's three work horses munching their allotment of hay. Peggy, a black cocker mix who was my constant companion, came to my side for a pat and a hug. All the animals were my friends and confidants, my entertainment and my education. The mother cat brought a mouse to her young and then gave their bath, even licking their behinds while the kittens chewed on the catch. I watched the rhythmical sideways motions of the cow's jaws as they patiently chewed their cuds. A mother's protective actions of her new calf gave me a sense of animal feelings, a respect for their instincts, and a camaraderie with them that stays with me yet.

Thinking of the hay reminded me of the labor involved in getting it into the barn, the straw on the stack, the oats in the granary, and the corn in the crib. For us kids it meant hours of hoeing thistles in corn, shocking grain, and loading and unloading hay. We complained, but learned first hand, "If you don't work, you don't eat."

Back to reality, I ran my hand over the wide porch rail caked with cracked paint. Hoisting myself up on it, I sat there with feet dangling. My eyes swept across the unkept lawn to a small patch of weeds, Pa's last attempt at gardening.

In my mind I could hear the sound of stone clanking against metal as Pa cleaned the soil from his hoe so many times in evenings past. The garden was much larger then. What we couldn't grow, we didn't eat. Like most children, I dreaded weeding onions and picking potatoes. Pa dug, we picked them up. I spent hours picking currants for jellies, and snapping beans to fill canning jars. There were beets to pickle, raspberries to can, and sweet corn and peas to freeze at the locker plant in Van Dyne. As a 4-H member I learned the best way to process all these treasures gleaned from the earth, and took pride in all the ribbons I won at the Winnebago County Fair. I can still feel the full, satisfied feeling it gave me.

As I sat on the porch rail in the spooky afterglow, another sound came to haunt me. It was the melodic tinkling of a cow bell. My Uncle Charlie down the road would have turned his Brown Swiss out to the woods for the night. His lead cow always wore a bell. I smiled as I thought of my cousin Irene and the fun we had.

Whenever I had time off from helping in the field or house, I biked over to Irene's. Our imaginations and the materials at hand gave us plenty to do. We walked around the straw stack to see who could find the most strings (twine that held the bundles before threshing). It took a sharp eye as twine and straw appeared alike. If we wanted to play house we made a "blue-print" on the lawn using rows of leaves or straw we raked up. Open spaces marked doorways. We were careful never to "step through" a wall.

In the fall Irene came as far as my driveway on her bike, and we rode together the next mile to the one-room Howlett School. We always got there early so we could get some games in before teacher rang the bell.

The church, the school, and the 4-H club were our education and our social life. Everyone knew everyone and everything they did, and everything their ancestors did for two generations back. If someone was missing at church on Sunday, we found out the reason why before we went home.

Now it was dark. I forced myself to leave the porch of memories and return to the job at hand.

Inside, I looked at the worn couch and the smudgy path on the carpet where Pa had shuffled to the bathroom so often, not always getting there in time. Behind the door was a sock. Where it once had a heel, Pa had pulled red yarn back and forth to close the opening. The words came back to me that I had heard so often, "Not much for looks, but hell for strength!"

For 88 years Pa had slept under this roof where he was born. For 88 years he has walked and worked the fields outside. He had followed in the footsteps of his father and the father before him, who emigrated from Germany to this town of Black Wolf. It had torn me apart the day I took him away. I can still see him clinging to the neck of the old neighbor who had come to say good-bye. Tears rolling from eyes that I had never seen cry. "I had wanted to die here," he said, "but what can you do?"

There wasn't really much left of value. Only the age of his possessions had made them valuable, and those real antiques had long since been bestowed on grandchildren.

On the bottom shelf of the nicked coffee table I noticed a German prayer book, left there from when he still could read. I picked it up. I couldn't read it, but I could understand what it had meant to him.

From the little built-in cupboard Mom had insisted he construct in the kitchen "for your tobacco mess" I gathered four fence post staples, his cheap pocket watch with the shoestring fob still attached, and a crinkled rusting Prince

Albert tin. Before I left, I picked up the sock. Treasures in hand, I went out into the night.

I locked the door behind me. I knew I would not be back.

Values have changed so that the 60 acres can no longer support a family. That kind of farming has died—in the wake of something called "progress." I don't know what will happen to the land. Whoever buys the place will have to remove what's left of most of the buildings. The house needs extensive remodeling.

Whatever changes come to it, no one can change the values I absorbed there: a sense of self worth; a respect for God, His land, His creatures, and His people; and a love for those common people.

I don't like to see death and I resist change. No, I won't be back. I want the farm to stay in my memory as it was; with cows in the woods, hollyhocks nodding their heads under the south kitchen windows, and Pa in the garden at dusk.

April, 1986

How Can I Forget You?

How can I say good-bye and forget you, my old farm?
    When my pores are filled with the dust of your land,
When my body is marked with the scars you have given me,
    When every time I see a sunrise or a hailstorm,
Scenes of your fields flash back through my mind.

How can I forget you, my farm?
    When my lungs cry out for your air
Free of vapor, fume, and smog,
    Only kissed by the sun
And refreshed by drops of rain.

How can I forget you when I hear a calf cry
    Or smell the aroma of fresh-mowed hay,
    . . . the memories come flooding back.

Once Upon A Farm

You made me feel inferior when my wardrobe
  Couldn't compare to corporate finery;
Yet you gave me sense of worth when I realized
  The milk I produced nourished life—not destroyed it.

How can I discredit you, my farm?
  When my whole life has been influenced
By the lessons you have taught me.

You took from me my strength and my youth,
  But you gave me back so much more:
Pride, fulfillment, and a value for life.

How can I forget you, my farm?
  When I see a seed push its fragile sprout of life
Through a crust of earth;
  Or watch the barn swallows return on time in April.

Then I remember the closeness I felt with my Creator
  Each day as I witnessed the miracle of life—
The goodness of the earth—
  Once upon a farm.

July, 1992

ORDER FORM

Please send me a copy of this book, *Once Upon A Farm.*

Name_____

Address_____

City, State, Zip_____

Send _____ copies at $12.95 each

Sales Tax
Please add 65 cents tax for books shipped to Wisconsin addresses.

Shipping
Book rate: $1.50 for the first book / .75 for each additional book

Payment
Total amount in check or money order to:

Lois Stark
Down-To-Earth Publishing
2302 Wall Street
Berlin, WI 54923

ORDER FORM

Please send me a copy of this book, *Once Upon A Farm.*

Name_____

Address_____

City, State, Zip_____

Send _____ copies at $12.95 each

Sales Tax
Please add 65 cents tax for books shipped to Wisconsin addresses.

Shipping
Book rate: $1.50 for the first book / .75 for each additional book

Payment
Total amount in check or money order to:

Lois Stark
Down-To-Earth Publishing
2302 Wall Street
Berlin, WI 54923

Lois Stark grew up on a small dairy farm in mid-Wisconsin. For 36 years she has been a farm wife and mother, taking part in all phases of farm life, from cleaning pens and daily milking chores to giving the invocation at a State Holstein Convention. Lois and her husband developed their Stark-Acres herd to one of the top producing Holstein herds in the state.

They continue to live on their 260 acre farm near Berlin, Wisconsin, with 50 cows and their offspring, numerous cats, and the dog, Bear.

239043